Mutual Empowerment

"Does marriage have a future in the post-patriarchal world now struggling to be born? Can there be Christian marriage no longer entangled in patriarchal patterns? Breazeale answers yes. But this will be possible only as we genuinely understand and repent of the ideas of gender, sexuality, bodiliness, relationality, and sin that have shaped past understandings of marriage. This book both guides us into such *metanoia*, such profound turning, through rethinking the theology that underlies practice."

John B. Cobb Jr.
Professor Emeritus, Claremont School of Theology

Mutual Empowerment

A Theology of
Marriage, Intimacy,
and **Redemption**

Kathlyn A. Breazeale

Fortress Press
Minneapolis

MUTUAL EMPOWERMENT
A Theology of Marriage, Intimacy, and Redemption

Cover image: *Yellow Leaves* by Georgia O'Keeffe, American, 1887-1936 (1928). Oil on canvas. Brooklyn Museum 87.136.6. Bequest of Georgia O'Keeffe. Used by permission.
Cover design: Ivy Palmer Skrade
Book design: PerfecType, Nashville, Tenn.
Author photo: Jordan Hartman
Readers will find additional materials on this volume for discussion, reflection, and further reading at fortresspress.com/breazeale.

Library of Congress Cataloging-in-Publication Data
Breazeale, Kathlyn A.
  Mutual empowerment : a theology of marriage, intimacy, and redemption / Kathlyn A. Breazeale.
    p. cm.
  Includes index.
  ISBN 978-0-8006-2039-4 (alk. paper)
  1. Marriage—Religious aspects—Christianity. I. Title.
  BT706.B74 2008
  261.8'3581—dc22
                              2008030531

12 11 10 09 08 1 2 3 4 5 6 7 8 9 10

CONTENTS

To the memory of my grandmothers:
Stella Feuillan Beverungen
and
Cynthia Walker Breazeale

PREFACE

Because men and women no longer face the same economic and social compulsions to get or stay married
as in the past, it is especially important that men and
women now begin their relationship as friends and build
it on the basis of mutual respect. You can no longer force
your partner to conform to a predetermined social role
or gender stereotype or browbeat someone into staying
in an unsatisfying relationship.

Stephanie Coontz[1]

While the current same-sex marriage controversy
has demanded public debate about the institution of marriage, the fact is that heterosexual
marriage is in trouble in the United States: 65 percent of
all marriages end in divorce,[2] and approximately one in five
adults has been divorced.[3] On average, every day more than
three women are murdered by their husbands or boyfriends
in the United States,[4] and recent research has identified
"male dominance in the family" and "belief in strict gender
roles" as two factors that increase the probability of perpe-
trating intimate partner violence.[5]

For many Christians, these alarming divorce and domestic violence statistics raise questions about their religious

beliefs and traditional marriage roles: What *is* marriage, anyway? What's a new and compelling vision for one of the most important relationships in life? What do I need to change or give up to make my own marriage relationship *authentic*? What does my marriage mean in my Christian commitment, and how does that correspond with traditional Christian ideas of love as submission or with notions of "headship" and "family values" advocated by Christian evangelists?

This book proposes a new paradigm of marriage as mutual empowerment and redemption through intimacy that is a compelling Christian vision for our time. Genuine Christianity is expressed through this new paradigm of marriage as mutuality that facilitates generosity and social transformation. As a component of redemption, Christian marriage based in mutual empowerment enables the creative transformation of the partners and their communities for the greater good. Intimate partnerships are one of our greatest opportunities for both redemption and sin because, as verified by quantum physics, relationality is an inescapable fact of existence. We are peculiarly vulnerable to the actions of the other, especially those in our closest personal and communal relationships.

This book develops concepts of God and power, sin and redemption, body and soul, and sexuality and spirituality. These concepts are alternatives to traditional understandings of Christian doctrines—doctrines that have been used to justify the dominance of husbands over wives and to deny church-sanctioned partnerships for lesbian and gay couples. While this book focuses on heterosexual marriage, it offers a partnership ideal that can be embraced by all couples.

Couples can work toward the ideal of mutual empowerment and redemption through intimacy by practicing relational power, adopting a concept of God that promotes intimacy, understanding sin as a violation of our interrelatedness, and conceiving a relationship of mutuality between body and soul and between sexuality and spirituality. Couples who embrace this ideal can enable the development of the greatest good for each other and their community.

This book opposes religious views of marriage that continue to advocate a marital hierarchy of husband over wife for two reasons. First, the failure of the dominant:husband/submissive:wife marriage model is evident in the current divorce and intimate partner violence statistics. Second, the traditional association of sin with the body, sexuality, and women has been used to label women as inferior and to condone violence against wives, making genuine intimacy between wives and husbands more difficult to achieve. This book also opposes the secular conception that marriage is shared self-gratification within an isolated consumer unit called the nuclear family. As Christians, marriage partners are called to extend their love and concern for well-being beyond themselves to include their communities. Furthermore, this book is based in the belief that relationality is the most fundamental aspect of existence. Couples and families do not exist in isolation. Rather, they are constituted by the networks of relationships in their lives.

This book offers an ideal for Christian marriage by developing basic theological concepts that underlie intimate partner relationships and by examining the implications of this ideal for social transformation. This book does not address all the practical questions of marriage in the larger framework of family, the variety of ethnic and other contexts in which marriage is concretely lived, economic issues, and how children alter all this. These questions have been well addressed by others.[6]

I am grateful to my community of support for accompanying me on the journey of bringing this book into being. This community includes John B. Cobb Jr. and Marjorie Hewitt Suchocki, who critiqued first drafts of this book manuscript and offered invaluable insights, and who continue to be unwavering in their empowering mentorship. Michael West, Fortress Press editor-in-chief, gave careful attention to details large and small, sparked with his wonderful sense of humor, and he enabled me to transform my ideas into this book. My colleagues in the Religion Department at Pacific Lutheran University provided a stimulating arena and strong, helpful responses to my work, especially Patricia O'Connell Killen, Samuel E. Torvend, Marit A. Trelstad, and Daniel J. Peterson. I am also indebted to longtime dear friends and conversation partners Gail A. Benson, Helene Talon Russell, and Linda Neese Sullender, and to my parents and siblings who never stopped believing in me. And for his ongoing inspiration, I am grateful to Jon Berkedal, with whom I continue to learn about mutual empowerment.

To aid readers in coming to terms with theological concepts and practical implications of this rethinking of marriage, I have composed, for each chapter of the book, some questions for reflection or discussion. I have also assembled some suggestions for further reading on each of the chapter topics. Readers will find them online at fortresspress.com/breazeale.

CHAPTER ONE

Rethinking Power
From Violence to Mutual Empowerment

> Any attempt to define love into the marriage relation runs the risk of ignoring or masking how power works within it.
>
> Adrian Thatcher[1]

Once upon a time, there was a young Christian woman engaged to be married. She loved the man who would become her husband, and one act of loving him was to change her name to his. Yet as the day of the wedding approached, she began to feel a deep sense of loss. By changing her name, she felt she was losing the self-identity she had carefully created for the first twenty years of her life. Her feelings of loss and sadness turned to anger and despair when she thought about how her name would disappear, for example, in the telephone book. In the future, she could not be found unless the person knew her married name. Yet her husband would continue to be as visible as he had always been. This did not seem fair. Although she did not have the terms to analyze her feelings, this young woman was beginning to "unmask" the power imbalance in traditional marriage roles.

For some women who become wives, this power imbalance leads to not only psychological anguish, but also physical violence. Pop singer Tina Turner "unmasks" how power turned to violence in her marriage and influenced her definition of love in her song "What's Love Got to Do with It?" A film by the same title tells the story of Turner's relationship with her husband, which included being beaten by him, and how she eventually found the courage to leave the marriage:

> I've been taking on a new direction
> But I have to say,
> I've been thinking about my own protection.
> It scares me to feel this way.
>
> What's love got to do, got to do with it?
> What's love but a sweet old-fashioned notion?
> What's love got to do, got to do with it?
> Who needs a heart when a heart can be broken?[2]

How serious is the problem of intimate partner violence and divorce in the United States? Intimate partner violence occurs in all population groups across the differences of race, class, and religion.[3] Every nine seconds a woman in this country is beaten by her husband or boyfriend,[4] and nearly one-third of women in the United States (31 percent) report being physically or sexually abused by a husband or boyfriend at some point in their lives.[5] These statistics are staggering and indicate that intimate partner violence violates *one in four women* in the United States. Similarly, *one in three first marriages* will end in divorce within ten years, and one in every five first marriages will end within five years;[6] 65 percent of *all* marriages end in divorce.[7]

Many Christians are disturbed by the magnitude of these statistics and are asking: What are the underlying reasons for the troubled state of marriage in the United States? How can we resolve this problem? Some fundamentalist Christians answer that the high rates of partner violence and divorce are caused by the lack of adherence to a Christian theology of marriage built on male headship and female submission. In contrast, I hold that the male headship/female submission model of marriage has been one cause of the problem, and the high rates of partner violence and divorce are evidence of the failure of this theology. The roots of the current marriage trouble can be traced both to misunderstandings of power in relationship and to misunderstandings of the Christian vision of redemption and the role of marriage within this vision. Therefore, I offer a new paradigm of Christian marriage.

In the current social chaos created by the breakdown of the male headship/female submission marriage model, authentic Christianity is manifest in this new paradigm of marriage as mutual empowerment and *redemption*, defined as creative transformation of the partners and their community toward the greater good. Mutual empowerment fosters redemption through deeper intimacy for the couple, generosity, and social transformation. "Intimate" has been defined as "intrinsic, essential; belonging to or characterizing one's deepest nature."[8] In seeking to make known the essential, deepest nature of Christian marriage, this new paradigm defines *intimacy* as a process of knowing and being known through the practice of relational power. By practicing relational power, partners are able to abandon the preconceived gender roles of male headship and female submission that diminish intimacy. These gender roles diminish intimacy because each partner values knowing only the characteristics of the other partner that conform to the role expectations. Abandoning preconceived gender roles and practicing relational power also reduces the possibility of intimate partner violence. As intimacy based on relational power develops, the ideal of mutual power sharing replaces traditional social ideals that sanctioned the husband's use of violence to enforce his wife's submission.

Marriage as mutual empowerment avoids the "power trap" in which the husband tries to control directly through dominance and the wife tries to control indirectly through submission. In the practice of mutual empowerment, both partners trust the process of the relationship enough to be open to the possibilities for good that neither partner could envision on his or her own. Thus marriage relationships based on mutual empowerment can provide more opportunities for the good to emerge than marriages based on the traditional dominance/submission model. The good that emerges from mutual empowerment can lead to redemption of the partners and the wider community.

Power, Domination, and Partner Violence

As one begins to analyze why the male headship/female submission marriage roles have broken down for many couples, as revealed in the high rates of partner violence and divorce, it becomes clear that marriage has been an unequal power relationship throughout most of Western history. The husband has held legal and religious power over his wife, and the violent use of this power was justified by the traditional gender roles of dominant husbands and submissive wives. Whereas these roles were sanctioned in the dominant Christian tradition, a new Christian marriage theology of mutual empowerment and redemption through intimacy must address the relationships between power, violence, and gender roles. How the power imbalance created by traditional marriage roles can perpetuate partner violence is evident when one reviews the history of wife beating in Western marriage and current social science research regarding gender roles and intimate partner violence.

During the Roman period, only upper-class men and women were allowed to marry, and these men had the power of life and death over their wives through the law of *pater familias* (father as head and master of the family).[9] In England, medieval- and Reformation-period husbands could exercise their power through the common law "rule of thumb," which gave a husband permission to beat his wife with a stick as long as the stick was no thicker than his thumb.[10] In this same period, "the right of chastisement" provided legal and religious sanction to husbands throughout Europe to use violence as punishment if their wives did not fulfill the submissive wife ideal.[11] In colonial America, one example of religious support for the submissive wife ideal is found in the New England Puritan catechism. Wives were encouraged to repeat this catechism that ended with "Mine husband is my superior, my better."[12] Furthermore, a husband who did *not* exercise his control over his wife could be "fined or ducked in the village pond."[13] Thus the battered wife had essentially no recourse to seek redress from either legal or religious authorities. Tragically, these attitudes continued into the twentieth century in two forms: the view that a wife could be raped by her husband was still thought to be ridiculous, and wife beating was not treated as a serious crime.[14] For example, in 1954 a Scotland Yard commander reported: "There are only about twenty murders a year in London and not all are serious—some are just husbands killing their wives."[15]

Legally, Western wives had virtually no identity separate from their husbands until the early decades of the twentieth century when women won the right to vote. For example, married women's civil status was nonexistent in English common law, and they were treated as minors according to the Napoleonic Code in France.[16] Until the late nineteenth century in England and America, therefore, the law considered husband and wife as one, and that one was the husband. Furthermore, this law of "coverture" was believed to represent the will of God.[17] Christian officials could quote Genesis 2:24 to support legal coverture: "Therefore a man leaves his father and his mother and clings to his wife, and they become one flesh." Many Christian leaders also held that wives should submit to their husbands based on their interpretation of biblical texts such as Ephesians 5:22: "Wives, be subject to your husbands as you are to the Lord."[18]

Thus the wife's duty was to obey her husband, and if she disobeyed, she deserved to be beaten. In the medieval period, some church leaders even argued that this beating had positive benefits for both the wife and the husband. For example, in the *Rules of Marriage* compiled by Friar

Cherubino of Siena between 1450 and 1481, the husband is instructed to "beat her [his wife], not in rage but out of charity and concern for her soul, so that the beating will redound to your merit and her good."[19] One ramification of these centuries of power imbalance between wives and husbands is the current problem of intimate partner violence.

A causal relationship between intimate partner violence and the power imbalance established by the roles of dominant husband/submissive wife has been verified by recent social science research. For example, in analyzing twenty years of research, Kantor and Jasinski write, "Wife beating is more common in households where power is concentrated in the hands of the husband or male partner. . . . In these households, physical violence may be used to legitimate the dominant position of the male."[20] Other researchers have also identified this connection between violence and the traditional male gender role of dominance. For example, Heise and Garcia-Moreno cite "male dominance in the family," "desire for power and control in relationships," and "belief in strict gender roles" as three relationship factors that increase the probability for the perpetuation of partner violence.[21] And in answer to the question of what causes men's violence against women, Harway and O'Neil theorize that "power and control are critical for explaining men's risk for violence against women" and that "men's and women's socialization, specifically gender-role socialization and conflict, predispose men to risk factors that can trigger violence against women."[22] O'Neil and Nadeau explain that when a man believes that having control and power over his partner is needed to validate his masculine gender role, the woman becomes an object for his manipulation. This objectification dehumanizes the woman, and the conditions are created in which violence becomes more likely.[23]

Yet O'Neil and Nadeau believe the connection between gender-role socialization and violence can be broken. They argue that men can learn how the traditional male gender role may socialize men to use violence to resolve conflicts with women; with this learning, men can develop alternative, nonviolent strategies for conflict resolution. The encouraging analysis here is that since men have *learned* to believe that using violence is normative in their interactions with women, they can also learn to discard this belief and replace it with nonviolent strategies. Furthermore, Harway and O'Neil propose that new models of masculinity must be developed "to replace sexist and restrictive notions of manhood," models that include "new conceptions of power and control."[24] One such new conception of power is offered by the Christian marriage theology of mutual empowerment developed in this book.

In contrast to analyzing the traditional male gender role, Nutt discusses how women's gender-role socialization predisposes women to become victims of partner violence. When girls and women are taught that they are less valuable than men, girls and women do not develop the self-confidence, self-respect, or assertiveness skills that could protect them from ongoing abuse. For example, consistent patterns in female gender-role socialization increase the possibility that women will become involved in an abusive relationship or have difficulty leaving such a relationship. These patterns include "the expectation of living through others and sacrificing personal needs for others," "feelings of passivity and learned helplessness," and "lower academic and career expectations."[25] These patterns demonstrate how a woman may come to believe she is less powerful than her male partner, and the lower expectations for academic and career achievement increase the likelihood that a woman will not have the financial power to support herself (and her children) should she leave the abusive relationship. The new model of Christian marriage as mutual empowerment offers a possibility for wives and husbands to overturn the traditional dominant husband/submissive wife roles and thus reduce the likelihood of partner violence in their relationship.

Relational Power and Mutual Empowerment

In contrast to the concept of power as dominance and control, marriage as mutual empowerment is based in the practice of relational power, the ability to influence *and* receive influence from others. Process theologians Bernard Loomer and Rita Nakashima Brock have developed the concept of power as relational.[26] Their insights are important for understanding how the new paradigm of Christian marriage as mutual empowerment can enhance intimacy to foster redemption for the partners and their community.

Loomer defines relational power as "the capacity both to influence and be influenced by others. . . . [It] involves both a giving and a receiving."[27] This definition of power as the ability to give *and* receive influence is different from the commonly understood definition of power as only the ability to influence others and different from the *Webster's Dictionary* definition of power as the ability to give *or* receive.[28] Loomer's definition of relational power as the ability to give *and* receive is important in the new model of marriage as mutual empowerment because both partners are empowered to influence and receive influence, rather than the traditional ideal that empowered the husband to influence through domination and the wife to receive influence through subordination. In a marriage relationship of mutual empowerment, both partners are expected to receive as well as give.

Relational power is also the capacity to sustain a relationship that can enable couples to develop a long-term marriage bond and counteract current divorce statistics. In this capacity, the power to influence and the power to be influenced are so "relationally intertwined" that it is essentially impossible to "isolate them as independent factors."[29] Because the power to give and the power to receive are almost indistinguishable, the focus is on the relationship, rather than on one partner or the other. Relational power is not a possession to be used by an individual. Rather, relational power is in the interactions of relating; it is "the bonds which create and sustain, and are recreated and sustained by relational selves."[30] The bond of marriage being created by the couple becomes the locus of empowerment, rather than the power held by either husband or wife. Focusing on creating the bond of marriage as the source of mutual empowerment dismantles the hierarchy of dominant husband over submissive wife to foster genuine intimacy.

Practicing relational power can facilitate intimacy because power as domination creates a barrier to deep loving by preventing mutual giving and receiving. If the partners always define giving as the power to control and receiving as the lack of power, then it is not possible to establish the "creative and strong love" that can develop from mutual giving and receiving.[31] Whereas "creative and strong" love is possible when the receiver has equitable power with the giver, this analysis of power and love invites couples to imagine creating a partnership of mutual empowerment that challenges the traditional roles of dominant husband and submissive wife.

The traditional gender roles of dominant husband/ submissive wife also inhibit intimacy because the authentic feelings and self-acceptance of each partner are suppressed as wives and husbands follow preconceived roles. These roles suppress authentic feelings because as we are socialized to behave according to the stereotype of dominance or dependency, we do not develop a clear sense of self due to the fusion of the self with the gender role.[32] This fusion creates an effective barrier to the genuine intimacy we could experience with each other, and both men and women suffer from this loss of relationship.

For example, social scientists O'Neil and Nadeau write regarding the man: "The tragedy of the power-oriented, controlling man is that he forfeits interpersonal and emotional flexibility and rarely gets his deeper emotional needs met."[33] Regarding the woman, journalist Heyn offers a similar analysis of the negative effects of the subordinate wife role. Based on her interviews with thousands of women in the United States, she argues that as a woman complies with the "good wife" ideal of submission, her authentic self is lost and this loss destroys the marriage relationship.[34] While I hold that both wives *and* husbands must take responsibility for authenticity to prevent the demise of their marriage, I do believe that Heyn offers a compelling analysis of how the submissive wife role can prevent married couples from developing intimacy. In contrast, practicing relational power provides a promising possibility for creating genuine intimacy as couples can redefine the roles of wife and husband.

One of the biggest challenges in redefining the ideal marriage roles for mutual empowerment may be practicing the power to receive. The wife may have difficulty because the power to receive is not passive submission, and the husband may have difficulty given the traditional dominant role of husbands. Arguments for the husband's dominance as "natural" have been supported by the well-established biological theory that male aggressiveness is caused by higher testosterone levels in men. However, recent research argues just the opposite: aggressive behavior elevates testosterone secretion.[35] The social conditioning that rewards males for being aggressive—for example, the expectation that husbands should rule over wives—provides the context for increased secretion of testosterone that can lead to violence. Thus physical differences between males and females that must be taken into account in working for full mutuality may be due to social conditioning, not biology.

Regardless of which theory one accepts to account for male aggression, intimate partners should strive to develop their ability to receive from each other because the possibilities for redemption can occur in the strength of one's power to receive. I am defining redemption as creative transformation toward the good. Loomer's argument that the "influence of the other helps to effect a creative transformation of ourselves and our world"[36] is a key point as I build a case for how couples can experience redemption through intimacy.

When couples practice relational power, the partners are actively open to being influenced by the other without either partner losing her or his sense of self-identity, and thus these couples avoid the fusion of self and gender role that prevents genuine intimacy as described above. The power to receive influence is found in one's strength to consider the values and desires of another without losing one's own identity and sense of self; in contrast to passive reception, one is openly active to including the other in one's own world of meaning and priorities.[37] Thus, practicing one's power to receive influence is in sharp contrast to the traditional ideal of the submissive wife who was admonished to passively obey her husband. In marriages of mutual empowerment, couples actively choose to be influenced by each other. Genuine intimacy develops as the partners receive influence from each other by engaging their authentic selves, rather than following preconceived gender roles. Because the power to receive influence is valued equally for the wife and the husband, the possibilities for redemption are enhanced.

Redemption through Intimacy

Commonly accepted definitions of "redeem" include "to free from the consequences of sin," "to free from what distresses or harms," and "to repair, restore."[38] In our current society, the high rates of intimate partner violence and divorce are two examples of the consequences of the sin of broken relationships that cause distress and harm to many women, men, and children. Couples practicing relational power redeem each other from the restrictions of gender roles and restore their relationship to the mutuality that God intended in the order of creation. God's intention for mutuality between women and men can be defended because the establishment of the husband's rule over the wife in Genesis 3:16 is the consequence of sin, not part of the original creation in chapters 1 and 2. And as Phyllis Trible argues regarding Genesis 2:18, the word translated as "helper" does not include the connotation of subordination in the original Hebrew.[39] Understanding mutuality as God's intention and defining redemption as creative transformation toward the good can encourage couples not only to redeem each other *from* the sin of a non-mutual relationship, but also to redeem each other *for* working toward the good of mutual empowerment. However, accomplishing this work is challenging because the practice of relational power requires giving up all efforts to control the relationship so that the maximum good can emerge.

The concept of redemption through intimacy builds on Loomer's position that "true good is an emergent from deeply mutual relationships."[40] Because mutuality is the condition for creating good, the good that could develop is diminished if either partner attempts to control the relationship. Efforts to control restrict "the worth of the relationship to the level of value which already exists,"[41] and the relationship is limited by one person's view of what the relationship should be. Loomer argues that even when love for the other motivates one to seek to control the other for the other's good, the exercise of unilateral power has the limitation of a preconceived good. The preconceived good is a limitation because it "often exemplifies the conscious or unconscious desire to transform the other in one's own image."[42]

For example, if I seek to transform you in my own image, I pressure you to suppress your authentic feelings, and intimacy is blocked. I have sinned against you by seeking to limit the possibilities for the self you are becoming and the possibilities for the selves we can become together. Using the example of marriage, Loomer describes how the possibilities for each partner emerge from the particularities of the partner relationship itself:

> A wife is not the occasion whereby a man actualizes husbandly possibilities that reside or subsist wholly within the confines of his enclosed selfhood. The husbandly and wifely possibilities of the respective partners are peculiar to and are created out of that particular marital relationship in which each helps to create the other. The more deeply mutual and creative the relationship, the wider the range of emergent possibilities for those participating in the relationship.[43]

Loomer's description of how wives and husbands create each other illuminates why the traditional dominance/submission marriage model offers fewer possibilities for redemptive intimacy than the relational power marriage model. As discussed above, the dominance/submission model provides preconceived roles for husbands and wives that limit the possibilities for the self that each partner can become. These roles not only limit the possibilities for each partner as an individual; they also limit the possibilities for who the partners could become in the particular relationship that they are creating together. Thus the preconceived roles limit the depth of mutuality necessary for the emergence of the true good that the marriage relationship could contribute for the redemption of the partners and the community.

Henry Nelson Wieman's understanding of human good and sexuality also informs the argument for redemption through intimacy and the definition of redemption as creative transformation toward the good. The source of human good is the "creative process" (Wieman's term for God), which always transforms the human mind toward the intrinsic good or "qualitative meaning."[44] Sexuality, more than any other aspect of human life, facilitates human capacity for creative transformation toward the good because the major life events that lead to experiences of increased meaning are occasions associated with sexuality: birth, adolescence, finding a life partner to love, marriage, and the birth of children.[45] However, the work of creative transformation is idealized in marriage: "The undreamed of transfiguration of a world hovers over every union of man and woman where love breaks the constraints of self-protective concern, opening the way to deepest appreciative interchange."[46]

Wieman may be over-romanticizing the practical potential of erotic love to change people's personalities. However, his vision of the relationship between sexual intimacy and redemption does provide an ideal for how couples can simultaneously experience redemptive intimacy in their partnership and work for redemption in their communities. Sexual desire to unite with another breaks down the resistance to human responsiveness necessary for the development of other kinds of love that can lead to transforming the world. Thus sexual love is possibly the most effective force for facilitating creative transformation.[47] As each partner risks moving beyond primary concern for the self to embrace the welfare of the partner, the couple enhances their possibilities for embracing the welfare of their community.

The concept of how marital intimacy can promote redemption for the partners *and* their community is based in Alfred North Whitehead's theory of internal relations—a theory that can be used to explain the larger and ultimate context of relationships in which marriage develops. Whitehead developed this theory from the principle that the most basic aspect of reality is relationships (rather than objects), and this principle has been substantiated by quantum physics. In contrast to the conception that humans are beings who *have* relationships, Whitehead argued that human beings (as well as every aspect of creation) are continually being constituted *by* our relationships. We are internally related to one another because we are comprised by our relationships with each other. According to Whitehead, no being exists in "isolated self-sufficiency."[48] While some may dismiss Whitehead's theory of internal relations as only an abstract philosophical theory, it is, as Loomer noted, a description of the common human experience of how "everyone and everything we encounter becomes part of the fabric of our lives. 'Relation' in the internal sense is a way of speaking of the presence of others in our own being."[49] For example, the self I am becoming is comprised of the relationships I have with my partner, family, and community. If I had been born into a different family, or chosen a different partner, or lived in a different community, I would have had different relationships and become a different self.

Accepting Whitehead's theory of internal relations develops our capacity for intimacy and self-affirmation in marriage because one realizes that one is not isolated from or above or below one's partner. Acknowledging the relational constitution of the self enables one to move toward intimacy because one is not acting out preconceived roles of dominance or submission that negate affirmation of the genuine self. As Brock explains, "In the personal awareness of self-in-relationships, we are empowered to respond and act toward intimacy instead of dependency and toward greater openness and self-affirmation instead of self-sacrifice."[50] The genuine self is affirmed so that one can receive the influence of another without losing one's self and thus increase the possibilities for creative transformation of self and world.

The world of relationality described thus far is beautiful in that it holds these opportunities for redemption through intimacy. Yet as Marjorie Hewitt Suchocki observes, this world is also "dangerous."[51] The danger arises from the fact that relationality is an inescapable fact of existence. Relationality makes us peculiarly vulnerable to each other as, for example, evidenced in the intimate partner violence statistics cited above. Therefore, our intimate partner relationship, one of the relationships that influences us most directly and frequently, is one of our greatest opportunities for both redemption and sin. I define sin as a violation of our interrelatedness that causes harm to oneself or to another. In this radically relational world, my partner and I not only influence the becoming of each other toward sin or redemption; we also influence the becoming of our community. Our personal and corporate identity is dynamic: just as we are shaped by external influences, so we impact that which is other than ourselves.

And as Loomer acknowledges, practicing relational power is an art that is very difficult to accomplish. The difficulty is not only in being willing to give up efforts to control the relationship as described above, but relational power also "requires the most disciplined kind of mutual encouragement and criticism. The creative openness to this type of relationship involves possibilities of the greatest advance and the greatest risk."[52] "Creative openness" to a nontraditional model of marriage is challenging and may be frightening for many couples. Because the traditional marriage model has endured for centuries with legal and religious sanctions, this model can offer a sense of security to wives and husbands by providing an established way of relating during our current time of rapid change. However, the current divorce and intimate partner violence statistics question the effectiveness of the traditional marriage model to provide security for either wives or husbands.

Other couples may dismiss the practice of relational power as a utopian ideal or as irrelevant in the real world. However, ideals and goals do make a difference in reality. For example, effective healthy eating and exercise programs demonstrate that new attitudes and skills can be learned that eventually change old habits and ways of relating. As with any lifestyle change, some couples may feel guilty if they fail to achieve the ideal in striving to practice relational power. Yet the practical goal for a couple is to realize the good they can accomplish given the social roles that have shaped them. Because the problem is culturally conditioned and individual couples cannot effect change by themselves, the new paradigm of marriage as mutual empowerment advocates cultural change supported by Christian teaching regarding mutuality in marriage.

Is This New Paradigm Christian?

Does Christian Scripture teach that wives should be subordinate to their husbands?[53] In Galatians 3:28, Paul declares,

"There is no longer male and female; for all of you are one in Christ Jesus." However, in Ephesians 5:22, wives are admonished to "be subject to your husbands as you are to the Lord." How can this conflict regarding the status of wives in Christian communities be resolved? Interpreting Ephesians 5:22 is critical in the new paradigm of Christian marriage as mutual empowerment because it is one of the verses most often used to validate the submission of wives as a Christian mandate.

One means of resolving the conflict between Galatians 3:28 and Ephesians 5:22 is to examine the larger context in which these verses were written. Ephesians 5:21—6:9 is part of the Household Codes, a group of texts including Colossians 3:18—4:1 and 1 Peter 2:18—3:7 that gives instructions for ordering the patriarchal family. These texts were written after 70 C.E., during a time when Christians were under great pressure to prove they were not undermining the patriarchal family structure that was the basis of Roman society.[54] According to Elisabeth Schüssler Fiorenza, women and men in the earliest Christian communities had practiced a "discipleship of equals." Their concept of discipleship was based on Jesus' sayings, such as his definition of family, "Whoever does the will of God is my brother and sister and mother" (Mark 3:35), and on Paul's proclamation of equality among men, women, and slaves (Gal. 3:28).[55] These earliest Christians did *not* adhere to the patriarchal family structure. Thus, as Clarice J. Martin demonstrates, the Household Codes in Ephesians, Colossians, and 1 Peter "reflect an attempt to restrict the enthusiasm of women and slaves" to reinstate the patriarchal household and justify this household as Christian.[56] Because the Household

Codes reverse the teachings of Jesus and Paul, a literal reading of these texts should not be the ideal for Christian marriage today.

However, if the admonition for "submission" in Ephesians 5 is interpreted as *mutual*, then this text does provide one scriptural basis for the new paradigm of marriage as mutual empowerment. There is a parallel between mutual deference and the practice of relational power as being open to receiving the influence of another. Recent biblical scholarship disputes the traditional translation of the Greek word *hupotasso* as "submission." For example, evangelical scholar Catherine Clark Kroeger has argued that *hupotasso* "contains the idea of mutual support and responsibility, as in Ephesians 5:21":[57] "Be subject [*hupotasso*] to one another out of reverence for Christ." She explains that in the Greek, there is no verb in verse 22. Therefore, the admonition to wives to "be subject" to their husbands in verse 22 must have the same meaning as the admonition to "be subject" to each other in verse 21, and *hupotasso* in verse 21 "clearly implies mutuality."[58] Kroeger argues that in the first century C.E., this admonition for mutuality between wives and husbands was in striking contrast to Roman marriage law in which the wife often remained under the authority of her father, who could remove her from the marriage at any time. In opposition to this legality that created marital instability, the New Testament encourages families to work together with the wife as "an integral part of the unit."[59] Within this culture of marital instability, the following verses (Eph. 5:23–24) that state the husband is the head of his wife just as Christ is head of the church describe how the wife is an integral member of the Christian family, rather than a person with

marginal status as in some Roman families. Kroeger concludes that the biblical mandate for "submission" of wives to
husbands is "a call not to oppression and loss of self, but to
meaningful bonding and accountability within a committed
relationship."[60]

The new paradigm of marriage as mutual empowerment based in relational power is continuous with Christian
teachings of mutual support between husbands and wives.
There is a correspondence between being actively open to
another to receive influence in relationships based on relational power and the admonition in Ephesians 5 that Christians be mutually responsible to one another. Furthermore,
the admonition for mutuality in Ephesians 5 provided the
possibility for marital stability in a context of cultural instability. Similarly, the practice of relational power, which is
defined in part as the power to sustain a relationship, provides the possibility for marital stability amid the current
cultural instability evidenced by the divorce rate and intimate partner violence statistics.

In contrast to Kroeger, Clarice J. Martin does not debate
the meanings of *hupotasso*; rather, she poses a more basic,
underlying question: "Should we continue to accept as binding a Christianized pattern of hierarchical domination in
the marriage relationship? Or is this a case—as with the
slave regulation in the *Haustafeln* [Household Codes] genre
[for example, Ephesians 6:5]—where a literalist interpretation of the 'letter' imposes an outmoded social ethos of
another period onto the contemporary church?"[61] Just as
most Christians today believe slavery is contrary to the
teachings of Jesus, we should acknowledge that the subordination of wives is also incompatible with Jesus' preaching

about relationships in the reign of God. For example, Jesus' core teachings to "do to others as you would have them do to you" (Matt. 7:12) and "love your neighbor as yourself" (Matt. 19:19) must certainly apply to one's closest neighbor—that is, one's intimate partner. These teachings of Jesus fundamentally alter all relationships, including relationships in the family. The new paradigm of Christian marriage as mutual empowerment is one model for incorporating Jesus' admonition of mutuality into the marriage relationship.

Christian Marriage for Personal and Social Transformation

The new paradigm of Christian marriage promotes personal and social transformation through mutual empowerment of marriage partners. As partners practice relational power, the "true good" that can emerge only in mutual relationships develops. Partners can experience redemption through the intimacy they have created by mutual giving and receiving, and by trusting, rather than controlling, the relationship so the maximum good can emerge. The good that emerges can lead to redemption, which I have defined as creative transformation toward the good, and this good can lead the couple to work for redemption in their community.

Mutual empowerment is advantageous for marriage partners because the power imbalance created by the traditional gender roles of dominant husbands and submissive wives is destructive in two ways. First, it increases the likelihood of intimate partner violence. This is more likely because the dominant husband may dehumanize his wife as an object for manipulation, and the submissive wife may be socialized to be a victim of violence because she believes she is less valuable and powerful than her husband. Second, the traditional power imbalance inhibits the development of genuine love and intimacy. Power as dominance over others creates a barrier to love because dominance prevents mutual giving and receiving. The traditional gender-role stereotypes of dominance and submission diminish the possibilities for genuine intimacy because each partner must suppress his or her own authentic feelings. Neither partner develops a clear sense of self due to the fusion of the self with his or her gender role.

In contrast, partners are empowered to experience redemptive intimacy through the practice of relational power because this practice releases each partner from preconceived power roles of dominance or submission. Through both giving and receiving, partners are free to express their authentic feelings, thus creating bonds of mutual empowerment and possibilities for genuine, redemptive intimacy. By expressing authentic feelings, each partner develops a clear sense of self. Thus each partner is empowered not only to give but also to receive the influence of his or her partner without the loss of self. This power to receive can lead to the redemption of self and community, as one is open to being influenced by and responding to the needs of others. Sexual love may be most effective in facilitating redemption because the sexual desire to unite with another breaks down resistance to respond to the needs of others. As each partner risks moving beyond primary concern for the self to embrace the welfare of the partner, the couple enhances the possibilities for embracing the welfare of their community.

Relational power is also defined as the capacity to sustain a relationship. For married couples, the bonds of mutual empowerment and intimacy created by authentic giving and receiving are expressed in the marriage bond. The marriage bond is the source of power for the couple to create their relationship, rather than either partner being empowered (or not) by his or her gender role. To sustain the relationship, each partner must give up efforts to control the process of the relationship so that the maximum good can emerge. The good that could develop is diminished when the relationship is limited by one partner's view of what the relationship should be, so both partners must trust the relationship enough to be open to the possibilities for good that neither partner could envision alone.

The claim that intimate partner relationships are one of our greatest opportunities both for sin and for redemption is based on Whitehead's theory that our personal and corporate identity is constituted by our relationships. This theory promotes the development of intimacy, because when one acknowledges oneself as constituted by one's relationships, one realizes that one is not separate from or above or below one's partner or one's community. Using this theory of personal and corporate identity formation, couples practicing relational power can simultaneously experience redemptive intimacy in their partnership and work for redemption in their communities.

The new paradigm of Christian marriage as mutual empowerment and redemption through intimacy is continuous with the teachings of Jesus and Paul. Jesus advocated relationships based on mutuality and love, and he defined family as those who do God's will, rather than persons ordered by patriarchal relationships. Paul proclaimed the equality of all persons in Christ. In the reign of God on earth, the hierarchy of husbands over wives is dismantled. The Household Codes should not be used to condone the subordination of Christian wives because these Codes are contradictory to the vision set forth by Jesus and Paul. In contrast to the Household Codes' reinstatement of the patriarchal family to comply with the structure of Roman society, the new paradigm of marriage as mutual empowerment has implications for transforming contemporary social structures that perpetuate sexism and racism.

The new paradigm of marriage as mutual empowerment is also continuous with recent biblical scholarship regarding the understanding of "submission." The admonition in Ephesians 5:22 for wives to "be subject" to their husbands should be understood as mutual accountability between wives and husbands due to the original wording of the Greek text. There is a parallel between mutual accountability and being actively open to another to receive influence in relationships based on relational power. Furthermore, just as mutual accountability provided the possibility for marital stability amid cultural instability in the first century C.E., a marriage based in relational power that sustains the relationship provides the possibility for marital stability amid cultural instability in the twenty-first century C.E. The next chapter further examines the practice of relational power by analyzing how one's concept of God can facilitate or impede the realization of relational power and redemption through intimacy in marriage.

CHAPTER TWO

God
From Impassibility to Intimacy

To respond to the fear often expressed about the defini-
tive character of marriage [. . . church leaders must
help people become aware that] the fidelity of the two
spouses and the indissolubility of their bond is modeled
on the fidelity shown by God in the indestructible covenant he himself made with humankind and is a source
of happiness for those it unites.

Pope Benedict XVI[1]

Marriage also reflects the image of God's covenant with
creation. As God's servant, I am called upon to perform
marriage ceremonies for couples like Nancy and Brenda
who show a sincere, loving commitment to God and to
one another. Marriage between two men or two women
can have all the qualities of marriage envisioned in
Scripture, mirroring God's relationship with us: fidelity,
love, progeny, family, community, companionship and
mutual support.

Rev. Janet Edwards[2]

A s these two contemporary news articles indicate, church leaders on both sides of the same-sex marriage debate can agree that Christian marriage mirrors God's nature and God's covenant with humans and all creation. Thus for Christian couples, the ultimate framework of married love is the being of God.

God and Marriage

As this chapter builds a case for how a couple's view of God increases their capacity to develop redemptive intimacy in marriage, Alfred North Whitehead's description of God's love as both giving and receiving is an ideal model for how partners can love each other:

> What is done in the world is transformed into a reality in heaven, and the reality in heaven passes back into the world. By reason of this reciprocal relation, the love in the world passes into the love in heaven, and floods back again into the world. In this sense, God is the great companion—the fellow-sufferer who understands.[3]

Whitehead offers an image of God in a reciprocal relation of love with the world. Whitehead's proposed intimacy between God and the world is opposite to the Greek philosophical view adopted by early Christian orthodoxy that God is impassible—or, in other words, God is "not capable of being affected or acted upon."[4]

Embracing a concept of a relational God can increase one's capacity for intimacy and facilitate the development of redemptive intimacy between couples striving to practice relational power in their partnerships.[5] This thesis is supported by five images of God: Whitehead's concept of the "primordial" and "consequent" natures of God, Sallie McFague's models of God as Friend and Lover, and Carter Heyward's conception of God as power in mutual relation. Each of these thinkers adopts a relational worldview, that is, a view of the world in which all beings, including God, are constituted by relationships. Not only does the world need God, but each thinker also works out how God needs the world. God's love is associated with *eros* (one of the Greek terms for love), broadly defined as the desire for unity or mutual relation with the other and the urge toward promoting the other's well-being.[6]

Embracing these conceptions of God enhances one's capacity for intimacy in relationships because these understandings of God's relationship to humans are intimate: God and humans participate together in creating the quality of life on this planet for all beings. In Whitehead's view, we participate as cocreators in God, becoming complete as we contribute to God's process of creating and saving the world. This intimacy between God and the world is expanded by McFague to include intimacy between those who comprise the world and share a vision with God to work for the well-being of all creatures. In defining God as our power in mutual relation, Heyward identifies the very being and becoming of God with the practice of relational power. Heyward's conception of God parallels Bernard Loomer's view that the "true good" emerges from deeply mutual relationships as discussed in chapter 1.

Understanding ourselves to be cocreators with a God who needs us and who invites us to be God's beloved friends can encourage us to risk creating genuine intimacy with a human partner grounded in relational power. As McFague asserts, the way we model ourselves is influenced by our models of God.[7] In the relational models of God analyzed below, couples are called to engage in relational power to redeem not only each other, but also the world. As couples practice relational power to develop deeply mutual relationships, the true good emerges and grows, thus facilitating redemption or creative transformation toward the good.

God and the Husband's Authority

Association of the nature of God with the role of the husband has been one of the primary justifications for the husband's power over his wife. This dominance of husband over wife, which reflects the dominance of God over creatures in traditional concepts of God, creates a barrier to the development of mutual empowerment and genuine intimacy. Thus the new paradigm of Christian marriage as mutual empowerment that challenges the dominance of the husband needs an alternative to the concept of God as an all-powerful lord ruling over all creation.

The association of the husband's authority with divine authority is based in traditional interpretations of biblical texts such as Ephesians 5:22: "Wives, be subject to your husbands *as you are to the Lord*" (emphasis mine). Rosemary Radford Ruether writes that historically, "the term 'lord' (*dominus*) was used simultaneously for God as Lord of the world, the aristocracy as masters of the lower classes, and finally the male head of the household as lord of his wife, children, and servants."[8] For example, Protestant reformer John Calvin equated marital compatibility with the wife "submitting her will to her lord in all things and he in turn caring for her."[9] More recently, in 1998, the Southern Baptist Convention affirmed the association of the husband's authority and divine authority with this resolution: "A wife is to submit herself graciously to the servant leadership of her husband even as the church willingly submits to the headship of Christ."[10]

The parallel between the role of the husband and the nature of God has also been expressed in the belief that only males bear the image of God, based on 1 Corinthians 11:7. This verse proclaims that women should cover their heads because women are "the reflection of man," while men are "the image and reflection of God." Augustine, Bishop of Hippo in northern Africa from 395 to 430 C.E., resolved the conflict between Corinthians 11:7 and Genesis 1:27 (male *and* female created in the image of God) by declaring that Genesis 1:27 refers to male and female *together* as one nature. He argued that while a woman alone does not bear the image of God, "the woman together with her own husband is the image of God."[11] Augustine's argument could be interpreted as affirming the status of wives over unmarried women, yet his argument also reinforced the association of husbands with God. The husband's role is sanctified because the husband has the power to transmit the image of God to his wife just as God transmits God's image to creation. Thus the husband's power over his wife can be interpreted as a reflection of God's power over creation.

Understandings of God's attributes and God's relationship to creation were incorporated into Christian theology from Greek philosophy. One of the big questions for classical Greek philosophers was the nature of change: Why do some things change and some things stay the same? Their answer was to propose two realms of reality: one was the perfect, timeless, unchanging realm of the divine, and the other was the imperfect, finite, changing realm of this world. Following this dualistic conception of reality, the deity was held to be "the supreme and ineffable principle of truth, beauty, and goodness . . . the timeless origin of all things."[12] Thus when early Christian theologians adopted these Greek philosophical categories of perfection, they conceived the Christian God as transcendent, eternal, infinite, omniscient, and immutable. God was also believed to be impassible. God could not be capable of being influenced, changed, or limited because such characteristics would make God less than perfect and God was, by definition, perfect in every way.[13]

However, this view of God adopted from Greek philosophy is incompatible with biblical images of God as loving, acting with regard for human welfare, and reacting to human behavior. For example, the Bible portrays God as loving humanity so much that God acts to redeem humanity, forgive those who repent, and empower those who are willing to spread the good news of God's love. From Adam and Eve to Prisca and Aquila, the biblical God is known as initiating and responding to relationships not only with individuals, but also with couples.[14]

The story of God's relationship with Adam and Eve, the first two human beings who were also a couple, has intrigued the Western imagination for more than two thousand years.[15] Mignon R. Jacobs names the dynamic quality of this relationship as she writes, "The lines are blurry between the Deity's control of the human and the possibility of the human affecting the Deity's plan."[16] Even though God's original intent for creation is altered by this first couple's disobedience, God continues to interact with succeeding generations of couples to accomplish God's purposes. For example, God intervenes in the marriages of Abraham and Sarah (Genesis 18 and 21)[17] and Mary and Joseph (Matthew 1 and Luke 1) to produce children.

In contrast, children are not mentioned in the texts about Prisca (or Priscilla) and Aquila. This married couple traveled and worked with Paul, and they established a house church in each location where they resided, including Rome, Corinth, and Ephesus. The fact that this missionary couple is mentioned six times in the New Testament (Rom. 16:3–4; 1 Cor. 16:19; 2 Tim. 4:19; and Acts 18:2, 18, and 26) demonstrates their prominence in the early Christian movement. Paul praises this couple because they "risked their necks for my life," adding that it is Prisca and Aquila "to whom not only I give thanks, but also all the churches of the Gentiles" (Rom. 16:4). However, as a missionary couple, Prisca and Aquila were not unique according to Elisabeth Schüssler Fiorenza, who argues that "partnership or couple-mission, not individual missionary activity, seems to have been the rule in the Christian movement just as in the Jesus movement."[18] For example, the missionary couple Andronicus and Junia were in prison with Paul, and Paul refers to them as "apostles" (Rom. 16:7).[19] Given Paul's descriptions of the depth of commitment demonstrated by Prisca and Aquila and Andronicus and Junia, one could surmise that these couples believed their relationship with

God empowered them to risk imprisonment and death to spread the gospel.

Intimacy and God's Love

The conflict between biblical images of God, such as God's intimate interactions with couples, and the Greek philosophical view of God as impassible is resolved to some extent by Whitehead's proposal that God has two natures: primordial and consequent. However, Whitehead's God is intimate with creation, not impassible, because God's responsive love pervades both natures as God creates and saves the world.[20] To emphasize how God's two natures are processes that relate God to human and nonhuman creation, I use two gerunds (a verb form that functions as a noun) to name God's natures: "creating" to replace "primordial" and "saving" to replace "consequent."

God's creating nature is somewhat similar to the Greek philosophical understanding of deity in that God's creating nature is eternal and unchanging. Yet the creating nature of God is also a process of order, novelty, and unrealized possibilities or "the unlimited conceptual realization of the absolute wealth of potentiality."[21] From this wealth, God orders the best possibility to each nonhuman and human coming into being in every moment of experience given the conditions of the moment. This ordering of possibilities is God's ongoing creation of the world or "creative love."[22] Whitehead implies that God creates the world out of love because God's creating nature is sometimes referred to as the "Divine *Eros*," defined as "the active entertainment of all ideals, with the urge to their finite realization, each in its due season."[23] As Divine Love, God's creating nature is a process by which God's infinity, the infinite source of ideal possibilities, becomes actual and finite in the world.[24] God's creating nature expresses God's unchanging love that orders the creation of the world so as to bring forth increasing value through the creatures. God does this by participating intimately in the coming to be of every creature, including every moment of human experience. Thus, for example, God is present in every moment of a couple's marriage, offering the best possibilities to the couple as they are developing their relationship.

While God's creating nature is "the primary action of God on the world," God's saving nature is determined largely by the actions of the world on God.[25] God's saving nature is incomplete. It originates through God's interaction with the world and develops as God responds to the world being created by God's creating nature.[26] Thus God is intimate with the world through God's necessary relationship with the world because the world is the origination and development of God's saving nature. Humans are intimate with God as they contribute to the growth of God's saving nature.

In Whitehead's notion of the saving nature of God, the hierarchical image of God ruling over creation is turned on its side; power flows from God to creatures *and* from creatures to God. We become cocreators with God, and we experience our relationship with God as a creative process. This experience of creative process with God can encourage marriage partners to risk overturning the hierarchical image of the husband ruling over his wife to develop a relationship of creative process with a human partner. This creative process includes the practice of relational power, the giving and receiving necessary for honest communication and empathy.

For Whitehead, God's goodness is expressed through God's responsiveness to the world. As God responds to both the positive and negative consequences of human actions, God's saving nature develops, a nature that is "consequent upon the creative advance of the world."[27] God seeks to advance the world through love because, although incomplete, God's saving nature is "determined" by God's "necessary goodness."[28] This goodness is expressed through Whitehead's understanding of how God acts to save the world: "The consequent [saving] nature of God is his judgment on the world. He saves the world as it passes into the immediacy of his own life. It is the judgment of a tenderness which loses nothing that can be saved. It is also the judgment of a wisdom which uses what in the temporal world is mere wreckage."[29] God receives not only "the love in the world" (see quotation on p. 28), but also "what in the world is mere wreckage." When God takes the wreckage of the world into God's "own life," God experiences the pain and suffering of humanity. In this way, God "is the great companion—the fellow-sufferer who understands."[30]

God's intimate companionship with the world that includes giving and receiving can be a model for how wives and husbands can strive to be companions through the quality of their responsiveness to each other. Process theologians John B. Cobb Jr. and David Ray Griffin have asserted, "God enjoys our enjoyments, and suffers with our sufferings. This is the kind of responsiveness that is truly divine and belongs to the very nature of perfection. Hence it belongs to the ideal for human existence."[31] This definition of God's perfection as including ultimate responsiveness is the opposite of the Greek understanding of divine perfection as static and impassible. Whitehead critiques the Christian tradition for the "idolatry" of creating God in the likeness of the rulers of Rome, Egypt, and Persia.[32] In contrast, Whitehead extols the image of God found in the man from Galilee who "dwells upon the tender elements of the world, which slowly and in quietness operate by love," a love that "neither rules, nor is it unmoved."[33] This image of God as portrayed by Jesus is an image of responsive love that can be a model for Christian couples. Whitehead believes that God's "infinite patience" is another image that is necessary to comprehend God's saving nature.[34] For couples, striving for patience is more conducive to developing intimacy than striving for either dominance or submission.

The use of Greek philosophical categories to define the God portrayed in the Bible was a choice made to meet the needs of the people in their time. As the early Christian theologians were formulating and systematizing the beliefs that would become orthodox Christian teachings, the incorporation of Greek philosophy was important to establish the emerging new religion as intellectually credible with the well-educated Romans. And the biblical narratives were unable to answer all the questions raised by the story of Jesus and the experiences of subsequent generations of Christians. Similarly, contemporary Christian couples seeking to know God as they are striving to create partnerships of mutual empowerment and redemptive intimacy can consider an alternative philosophy, one that is more compatible with biblical images that portray God as intimately related with the world. I have offered Whitehead's philosophy as an unusually rich example.

The image of an omnipotent, impassible God ruling over creation has been used to support the traditional hierarchy of husbands ruling over wives. In contrast, the image of God becoming complete through a reciprocal relationship with the world can support couples striving to develop intimacy. The distance of God as ruler is overcome by the intimacy of God as companion, a companion who interacts with the world to create and save the world through patient, responsive love.

Intimacy and God as Lover

McFague expands Whitehead's conception of reciprocal love between God and the world to include reciprocal love between the creatures who comprise the world that God loves. If God is the lover and the world is the beloved of God, then as we creatures receive God's love, we must love the world—that is, each other—in order to return God's love.[35] Thus McFague's model of God as lover of the world can increase our capacity for intimacy because we can love God only through loving each other. As the writer of 1 John 4:20 declares: "Those who say, 'I love God,' and hate their brothers or sisters, are liars; for those who do not love a brother or sister whom they have seen, cannot love God whom they have not seen."

Similar to Whitehead's conception of God as "Divine *Eros*," God's love is associated with *eros* in the model of God as lover developed by McFague. God is the power of love that moves throughout the cosmos, and God's desire is "for unity with all the beloved."[36] Traditional Christian understandings have defined the beloved as an individual in relationship with God.[37] In contrast, McFague posits the world as the beloved of God within her definition of the world as God's body.[38] God loves the world "not with fingertips but totally and passionately, taking pleasure in its variety and richness, finding it attractive and valuable, delighting in its fulfillment."[39] In this context of the world as God's body, the beloved of God is the whole world that includes all creatures. God loves all creatures in the world equally and desires unity with all the diverse aspects of creation; no one aspect is singled out as more worthy or deserving of God's love. When applied to married couples, the hierarchy of the husband's role as closer to the divine than the wife's role is discredited, as there is no hierarchy in God's love for the world.

Similarly, we should return God's love by loving the world—God's body—not by loving God in a one-to-one individual relationship. Following God's way of loving, we too should love the world as "attractive and precious, valuable for its own sake. . . . [The] beloved cannot be God alone: it must also be the world that is the expression of God and that God loves."[40] Building on Whitehead's conception that describes how humans are intimate with God by participating in the development of God's nature, McFague's model describes how creatures are intimate with each other as we love God by loving the world.

In McFague's model of God as lover, our capacity for intimacy increases, because as we love the world, we respond to a God who grows and changes and needs the world. As Christians, our response to this growing, changing God as portrayed in the Bible can be a model for how we respond to each other. Similar to Whitehead's argument that the responsive love of God is imaged in Jesus, not imperial rulers, McFague uses biblical images to support her claim that God as lover needs the world: "Neither the covenantal God of the Hebrew Scriptures who pleaded with Israel to be his faithful partner nor the compassionate God of Jesus of Nazareth who healed the sick and cast out demons is an unmoved mover or absolute monarch entirely outside the circle of need. Need, of course, implies change and growth."[41] These images of a growing, changing God who needs the world can provide support for couples striving to develop intimacy, because intimacy is fostered as partners are willing to respond with compassion to the other partner's growth and change. All couples in long-term relationships face the inevitable changes brought by time. Marriage is willingness to risk that partners will grow and change in ways that continue to be compatible. Couples who take this risk can find support in believing in a God who is growing and changing with them.

Finally, embracing the concept of God as lover who needs the response of the beloved can facilitate the development of redemptive intimacy. As argued in the previous chapter, intimacy can become redemptive for couples striving to practice relational power because the true good that emerges from deeply mutual relationships can lead to the creative transformation or redemption of the partners and the world. When we believe that God needs us, we can be further motivated to assume that we are responsible for the world.[42] As McFague writes, "In the traditional view of redemption, something is done for us; here we are asked to join the work."[43] The belief that God needs us to take responsibility to work for the redemption of the world supports couples who are striving to develop a deeply mutual relationship that is open to the needs of each other and the world. In the mutual responding to each other and to God, the possibilities for good are not limited by what either partner could imagine on his or her own, and thus the possibilities are greater for developing redemptive intimacy.

Intimacy and God as Friend

Intimacy and friendship are associated in the English language, as "intimacy" is from the Latin *intimus,* meaning "close friend."[44] McFague defines friendship as "a bonding of two by free choice in a reciprocal relationship."[45] Therefore, her model of God as friend reinforces the reciprocity that is necessary for couples to develop redemptive intimacy. When applied to marriage partners, the inclusion of freedom in this definition also implies that the quality of friendship between wives and husbands is enriched by freedom from gender-role stereotypes.

McFague's definition of friendship focuses on free choice and reciprocity, not equality, which informs her powerful assertion that humans can be friends with God. McFague supports her argument by appealing to the relational worldview, a view also posited by Whitehead with his theory of internal relations (as discussed in chapter 1) and verified by quantum physics. If relationships are the most fundamental aspect of all life, then "in some extended sense" humans can be friends with both nonhuman life forms and the divine life of God.[46]

Although the bonding of two friends is reciprocal, it is not exclusive. They share a common interest or vision that not only unites them, but also opens the friendship to the world. In friendship between humans and God, this common vision "cannot be overstated, for it frees friendship from the self-absorbed individualism of its classical roots."[47] In our time, the common vision in friendship between human beings and God is "the well-being of the earth."[48] If couples adopt this model of God, their friendship with God will engage them with the needs of the world. Couples can be motivated to join with other individuals and groups who are working on behalf of our planet because dedication to a common vision is not limited to two persons.[49] As friends of God, the couple's ability to develop redemptive intimacy is increased because the couple is creating deeply mutual relationships with God and the world, as well as with each other. As couples develop these reciprocal friendships, they move beyond "self-absorbed individualism" to mutual giving and receiving.

What does it mean to be a friend of God and the world? McFague answers, "To befriend the world is to be its companion—its advocate and partner."[50] While both Whitehead and McFague image God as companion in God's relationship with the world, McFague extends this type of intimacy to define humans' relationship to the world as well.

The word *companion*, from the Latin *panis*, meaning bread, originally referred to persons who ate bread together.[51] Jesus' invitation to table fellowship is a symbol of God's friendship with humanity because, through Jesus' actions, God invites us as friends to eat together.[52] The table fellowship modeled by Jesus is also a symbol of developing friendships with others, including those whom our society devalues as outcasts. In this model of God as friend, celebrating the Eucharist becomes a ritual in which couples can affirm their intimate companionship with each other and with God, and in which they can be reminded of the possibilities of being companions of the world, of reaching out to those outside their relationship as a couple. As the couple shares their resources, their marriage can become a form of table fellowship in which they offer hospitality to each other and to the world.

Humans should be companions or friends of the world because, as stated in Genesis 1:27, humans bear the image of God, who in this model is the friend of the world. Thus bearing the image of God is an invitation to join with God as friends to work to fulfill God's vision for the well-being of the world.[53] For marriage partners, this invitation is extended to both husbands and wives, and each bears equal responsibility to respond. To bear the image of God is an opportunity for friendship with God and the world, not a quality that the husband transmits to his wife.

Finally, the nature of God as friend is also characterized as the One who sustains the world, "who bears the weight of the world, working for its fulfillment, rejoicing, and suffering with it, permanently."[54] This image of God's friendship as enduring can be an inspiration to married couples seeking to deepen their capacity for intimacy through their long-term relationship. In a relational world, couples don't just *get* married; rather, they *become* married over time. Marriage is more than a legal commitment; marriage is a process that develops as the two partners freely choose each day to fulfill their commitment to each other over time. This increasing depth of commitment cannot be achieved in one day during a wedding ceremony. Embracing the sustaining power of God's friendship with the world can help couples as they strive to sustain this kind of intimate friendship with each other.

Intimacy and God as Power in Mutual Relation

God as Power

In contrast to McFague's models of God as lover and friend, Heyward conceives of God as power. God is "our power in mutual relation"[55] or "right relation."[56] God is the source of our power to be alive, and God empowers us to live our lives in relationship with others.[57] And yet, paradoxically, God is not only the source but also the result of relationships that are mutual. Similar to Whitehead's conception of how God's saving nature develops, you and I create the ongoing life of God in Heyward's view. As we practice relational power, God, "the sacred power," becomes present as we are becoming ourselves in mutual relationships.[58] And similar to McFague's God as lover who needs the world, Heyward's God needs us, "her friends, to bring her to life and help nourish her life on the earth. She is being born among us, and yet she is seldom fully present, fully herself. To that extent, she is not yet but becoming."[59] Furthermore, the practice of relational power is how we come to know God and God's love, because relational power is "the root of our theological epistemology."[60] Thus for God to be fully present and for us to know God's love, we must risk developing relationships of mutuality. The new paradigm of marriage as mutual empowerment then becomes one of the greatest opportunities for God's presence to be fully realized on earth.

The conception of God as power in mutual or right relation changes the definition of the right ordering of power in the institution of marriage. The couple's relationship develops as each participates in a matrix of power *with* God, rather than conforming to the traditional hierarchal model in which power flows *from* God to the husband and then from husband to wife. Husbands and wives have equal access to becoming empowered by God. Opportunities for redemptive intimacy increase because through mutuality, the couple shares in creating God's presence in their relationship and community, rather than appeasing God through fulfilling the role of dominance or submission.

In contrast to ordaining relationships of dominance and submission, Heyward's God is embodied when humans cocreate mutual relationships. Relationships become "resources of growth" as God empowers us to act "joyfully" to liberate ourselves and all creatures "from bondage to wrong relation."[61] One of these wrong relations is the traditional order of creation that placed husbands over wives. Restored to the right relation of mutuality, wives and husbands can embody the Sacred in their marriage. When we are creating right relation, the Sacred is embodied as we are "acting with one another as resources of the divine Spirit."[62] Intimacy can be facilitated as wives and husbands share equally in being resources for each other, rather than only one of the partners being responsible for the spiritual welfare of the couple.

The embodiment of the Sacred is also associated with the erotic and mutual empowerment. Heyward defines the erotic as "the sacred/godly basis of our capacity to participate in mutually empowering relationships."[63] We most fully experience the embodiment of God's love through the erotic; it "is the source of our capacity for transcendence, the 'crossing over' among ourselves, making connections between ourselves in relation."[64] In this view of God's love, the erotic, and transcendence, the couple's love for each other is not isolated. Similar to McFague's conception of how humans participate with God as lover, the couple's capacity for intimacy is enhanced because through loving each other they also participate in God's love that extends throughout creation. The couple's love for each other transcends the bonds of their relationship so that their intimacy can become redemptive not only with each other, but also with their community. These possibilities for redemption can occur because our experiences with the erotic as sacred lead us "to know ourselves as holy and to imagine ourselves sharing in the creation of one another and of our common well-being. . . . We become resources with one another of a wisdom and a pleasure in which heretofore we have not dared believe."[65] By accepting this concept of the erotic as sacred, the couple's intimacy becomes a means through which they can know themselves as holy as they contribute to the well-being of God, each other, and their community.

Finally, similar to Whitehead's conception of God's two natures as process, Heyward argues that for both God and humans, the acts of "creation/creative" and "liberation/liberating" are "sacred process" and "relational empowerment." These acts are not separate, but are "at once creative and liberating, sensual and sacred."[66] To imagine God as a sensual and sacred process of relational empowerment offers an opportunity for couples to consider their marriage as a form of participation in this process. This participation invites an attitude of openness to the future. The couple's capacity for intimacy is enhanced by focusing on unknown possibilities of growing together in this process, rather than either partner imposing his or her own vision of what the relationship should be on the other.

Mutuality as Process

Logically following her conception of God as process and "our power in mutual relation," Heyward defines mutuality as a process in which "each participant in the relationship is called forth more fully into becoming who she is—a whole person, with integrity."[67] This definition of mutuality dismantles the traditional stereotypical roles of wife and husband as the ideals for a complete marriage. Each partner is considered to be becoming a whole person, rather than being "the better half," a person fulfilling one role who requires the other role to be complete. Freed of predetermined roles that inhibit the full becoming of each other, the couple has an increased capacity for intimacy.

Mutuality can be understood as a process of becoming because mutuality is dynamic. As mutuality is shaped, grows, and changes "with/in the relationship, . . . we become bearers with one another of the justice of God. Not perfectly, but authentically."[68] The shape of mutuality for married couples develops and changes as the couple responds to the contingencies of married life—for example, issues of employment, children, aging, and the needs of their extended families and community. As mutuality grows, so do the couple's opportunities for redemption through intimacy because their mutuality empowers them to manifest authentically God's justice, or "right, mutual, relation,"[69] with each other and with their community.

Yet this process of becoming in relationship to manifest God's justice is not easy, because mutuality is not merely reciprocity or the suppression of differences, nor is it without anger or conflict or fear. Rather, mutuality is filled with tension because it is a "process in which two or more people are struggling to share power between/among ourselves."[70] Mutuality requires "risking *through* fear,"[71] especially the fear "to love and be loved for who we really are,"[72] and developing our ability to "recognize and honor the differences we bring to our common ground."[73]

Honoring differences is particularly important for Christian couples who have been offered the marriage ideal of becoming one based on Genesis 2:24, "The two shall become one flesh." Yet the "one" has usually been the husband because the wife was to submit to the husband, a submission reinforced by legal statutes. One historical example is the argument used against giving women the right to vote. Because the husband was considered the head of the wife, the husband's vote was considered to include the wife's vote.[74]

A contemporary example of the two becoming one is the popular practice of lighting a "unity candle" during Christian wedding ceremonies. The bride and groom light this large candle from two smaller burning candles and then extinguish these two smaller candles. In the new paradigm of marriage as mutual empowerment, couples might leave the two smaller candles burning to symbolize their ongoing recognition of the differences that each partner brings to the marriage. Recognizing the differences between partners enhances the development of intimacy, because knowing the differences is part of knowing who the other person really is or, more accurately in a relational world, who the other person is becoming. When these differences are trivialized or ignored, a distorted sense of unity is created. The unity is distorted because it is not based on the fullest understanding of each partner for the other.

Honoring the different qualities of each partner facilitates the development of a mutuality that is not necessarily the same as equality. Mutuality, not equality, accommodates the contingencies of marriage because each partner does not bring equal gifts and strengths for every aspect of the relationship.[75] While equality suggests the attainment of the same rank for each person, mutuality "signals relational growth and change and constitutes an invitation into shaping the future together."[76] Thus mutuality in marriage is an invitation for couples to strive toward God's justice of right relation, rather than equity. Furthermore, the circumstances of daily life make it difficult to maintain equity or a fifty-fifty balance in giving and receiving. Most often, the balance will be sixty-forty or even eighty-twenty, yet the justice of mutuality requires that the same partner is not always giving more and receiving less.

Although mutuality is not the same as equality, developing mutuality often includes resolving inequality.[77] In the process of mutuality, "the energy for domination/submission is transformed erotically into power for sharing. Mutuality is a way of redirecting wrong relational power."[78] In the Christian tradition, inequality has been the dominant model for marriage proposed as God's will. Thus contemporary Christian married couples who adopt the understanding of God as power in mutual relation will have to revise the model they have been given. They will have to negotiate how they will redirect the wrong relational power of dominance and submission. Because mutuality is a process of justice empowered by God for calling forth the best possibilities in shaping the future,[79] the nature of mutuality cannot be predetermined or imposed from outside of the relationship. Thus mutuality in marriage will not look or be exactly the same for every couple. Rather, mutuality will develop from the specifics of the couple's relationship as these specifics change over time.

Intimacy and Mutuality with a Relational God

> Thus, the metaphors of God as king, ruler, lord, master, and governor, and the concepts that accompany them of God as absolute, complete, transcendent, and omnipotent permit no sense of mutuality, shared responsibility, reciprocity, and love (except in the sense of gratitude).
>
> Sallie McFague[80]

The five conceptions of a relational God examined in this chapter do permit "mutuality, shared responsibility, reciprocity, and love" that is more than gratitude. These conceptions suggest implications for intimate partner relationships, especially partners who are married. Redemption (or creative transformation toward the good) through intimacy is facilitated by adopting the conception of a relational God with the following three characteristics.

First, the nature and action of God are described with words that connote intimacy. These words include *companion, fellow-sufferer, lover, friend, erotic power,* and *mutual relation.* Mutual relation is also right relation or God's order of creation. Second, God's intimate relationship of love with the world is revealed through defining God as a powerful yet incomplete process of mutuality, possibility, and need. God needs the world to contribute to God's becoming and to work with God to save the world, to promote the well-being of the planet. God is growing and changing as God receives the world and responds with love to continue creating and saving the world. God is creating the world by offering possibilities for the good of the couple and the world that could not be imagined or possible without God. God is saving the world as God is in the process of developing deeply mutual, loving relationships that engage the couple with God, with each other, and with the world. Third, God empowers humans to strive for reciprocity and mutuality, not equality—to imagine how humans can respond to the inequalities in their relationship with God and with each other. Thus in the order of creation of this relational God, the hierarchy of husband over wife is dismantled not just to achieve equality, but to strive for mutuality that requires both partners to be free from preconceived gender roles.

By adopting the understanding of a relational God, the couple experiences an increased capacity for intimacy, for intimacy between wives and husbands in Christian marriage reflects God's intimate relationship with the world. Marriage is a form of participation in the becoming of God, a relationship of creative process with a human partner modeled on a relationship of creative process with God. Over time, couples become married (in more than a legal sense) as they freely choose each day to fulfill their commitment to one another. Couples offer each other a responsive, patient companionship following God's companionship of giving and receiving love. In response to God's love, couples love God by loving each other and the world. As a manifestation of this love, Christian marital intimacy is a form of table fellowship in which couples provide not only for each other, but also for those in their communities. As two persons equally marked with the image of God, the couple responds to God's invitation to offer hospitality to each other and to the world.

Finally, one ideal of Christian marital intimacy is mutuality in all areas of the relationship. The couple's mutuality develops from the specifics of the couple's relationship that change over time as partners honor each other's differences and respond with compassion to each other's growth and change. Couples are invited to strive toward God's justice, rather than equity, and to negotiate how to redirect the wrong relational power of dominance and submission. Through mutuality, marriage embodies the Sacred as God empowers the couple to redeem each other from wrong relation, a relation that limits the possibilities for the full becoming of each partner. The next chapter examines how theological conceptions of body, soul, sin, and sexuality shaped the development of the wrong relation of dominant husband/ submissive wife in the Western Christian tradition.

CHAPTER THREE

A Legacy of Female Subordination and Violation

Anglican leaders gathered in Dar es Salaam, Tanzania, on Thursday to discuss the problems that have ensued since 2003 over the consecration of Bishop V. Gene Robinson by the U.S. Episcopal Church, their liberal stance on same-sex unions, and the fact that they've yet to repent on either. The Anglican Church is fighting to keep its warring churches from dividing its 77 million members, a split that would be the worst in Anglican history.

Purple Pew News[1]

I don't know what the big deal is about petitions being circulated in churches. No one's being forced to sign the petitions, even if your pastor or bishop thinks it's a good idea. . . . If the idea of abortion petitions being circulated in church bothers you, find a church that's more to your liking. There are many more religions and churches than there are political parties, so you have plenty of choices where to plant your faith.

Randy Rasmussen[2]

Let's be clear from the beginning: the problem of sexual abuse by clergy is happening within every faith tradition;

the victims are boys and girls, women and men; clergy offenders include every race, gender and sexual orientation. For at least the past twenty years, we have known about sexual abuse by clergy. Some judicatories have moved to address it and prevent it. Others have ignored the disclosures, moved offenders to new venues, and allowed abuse to continue.

Marie M. Fortune[3]

Christian denominations in the U.S. are currently plagued with controversy over homosexuality, abortion, and evidence of sexual abuse by clergy, all taking place within a culture pervaded by divorce and domestic violence. This is an important time, therefore, to critically reexamine the roots of Christian doctrines regarding sexuality and marriage. Examining the past provides evidence for why alternative understandings of body, soul, sin, and sexuality are needed. The association of sin with the body, sexuality, and women has been used to verify that women's nature is inferior and to condone violence against wives, thus making genuine intimacy and mutual empowerment between wives and husbands more difficult to achieve in Christian marriage.

Three successive stages in the appropriation of the traditional doctrines of body, soul, sin, and sexuality to justify female subordination and violation can be summarized in the work of one most influential thinker in each stage: Augustine of Hippo, Martin Luther, and Sigmund Freud. The hierarchy of soul over body and males over females in the theology of Augustine and Luther is supported by their understandings of sin and sexuality. These hierarchies are elaborated by Augustine, modified by Luther, and verified with "scientific proof" by Freud in his psychology of women. Although Freud is not specifically a theological thinker, I have chosen him because his work effectively demonstrates how the new authority of science perpetuated the same old theological views: women's nature is inherently inferior and therefore men should dominate over women, even if this domination includes violence.

Augustine, Luther, and Freud are complex thinkers from whose work a variety of conclusions can be drawn. The focus here is how their conceptions of body, soul, sin, and sexuality, with particular attention to their use of metaphor and analogy, provided a basis for asserting the inferiority of women's nature and advocating for dominant husbands and submissive wives. They all justified the use of violence to maintain the wife's submission and developed their theories of female subordination in contexts in which actual women were challenging this subordination. Examining these contexts illuminates how these thinkers' views about women, sin, body, and sexuality function within the larger social framework of understandings about the roles of husbands and wives, and in particular the use of violence to maintain these roles.

Early Christianity: Augustine

Augustine's work is important because his ideas about the nature of body, soul, sin, sexuality, women, and men have set the dominant standard in the Western Christian church for more than fifteen hundred years.[4] Relevant to developing a new paradigm of marriage as mutual empowerment is how Augustine justified the subordination of wives to husbands.

He associated female sexuality with sin and argued that female bodies do not bear the image of God. Furthermore, his views on subordination provided a basis for condoning the practice of wife beating.

Women's Sexuality, Sin, and Honor

Elaine Pagels contends that Augustine, influenced by his own experience, makes a "leap that identifies sexual desire itself as evidence of—and penalty for—original sin."[5] In contrast, I hold that rather than through a "leap," Augustine arrives at his position regarding uncontrolled sexual desire and sin through a series of rational steps based on his understandings of body, soul, sin, and sexuality.[6] He retains the traditional Greek hierarchy of soul over body, yet he rejects the classical concept of the body as the source of sin and evil. Rather, Augustine incorporates the Judeo-Christian notion of bodily goodness with his theory that sin is located in the will of the soul divided against itself, not in the body's physicality. Due to sin, the soul's will is unable to exercise its proper control of the body—a lack of control that is most obvious in uncontrolled sexual desire. Thus sin is intimately associated with sexuality. Furthermore, amid controversy about women's subordination, Augustine posited that female sexuality is more tainted with sin than male sexuality in order to support his case for the subordination of women to men and, in particular, wives to husbands.

The basis of the controversy about women in the fourth- and fifth-century Christian communities was the theological conception that although women and men are spiritually equal, women are temporally subordinate to men due to the effects of Eve's sin. Following Eve, every woman must bear her children in pain and be subject to the rule of her husband (Gen. 3:16). However, many Christian women who practiced asceticism were interpreting their asceticism as liberation from the effects of Eve's sin; virginal and ascetic women were claiming that the denial of their bodies freed them from the twofold curse of Eve: childbearing and male domination.[7]

As a bishop of the church, Augustine refuted the women's claim that asceticism freed them from subordination to their husbands in his undated letter to Ecdicia, a wealthy African matron who had obtained a consent of continence from her husband. Then, without his consent, she gave away her clothes, gold, silver, and money to two wandering monks. Augustine responded with reproof, instructing her to apologize and beg forgiveness from her angry husband. Augustine declared that as a wife, Ecdicia should have been subject to her husband in everything, especially since they were both Christians.[8] As Elizabeth A. Clark observes, "For Augustine, Christian commitment apparently implies a greater, not a lesser, degree of wifely submission."[9]

To provide a Christian basis for justifying the subordination of women to men, Augustine interpreted biblical texts to prove women's inferiority to men and to associate female sexuality with sin. Augustine argued that women are inferior by nature with his attempt to reconcile the conflict between Genesis 1:27 (simultaneous creation of male and female) and Genesis 2:7 (Adam created first): women are spiritually equal, as in Genesis 1:27, and temporally subordinate, as in Genesis 2:7. Augustine postulated that in Genesis 1:27, God created the cause and potentiality of every living thing, including Adam and Eve. This creation is not in time; rather, cause and potentiality are "primordial seeds" (similar to Plato's "forms") floating in the realm of the eternal. In Genesis 2:7, however, these seeds were incorporated in time and matter when "Adam" was created out of the dust of the earth. Later in Genesis 2:18, "Eve" was created from his rib as "helper." To be second is to be inferior, and thus Augustine "proves" woman's "natural" inferiority.[10] By defining woman's nature as "naturally" inferior to man's, Augustine and other patristic theologians could extol the virtues of virginity and continence in marriage as enabling women to overcome their inferior nature while demanding that actual women remain subordinate to men.

Augustine also used the creation story of Eve as "helper" in Genesis 2:18 to associate female sexuality with sin. Augustine could not imagine woman's role as anything other than procreation because he believed a male would be a better "helper" for tilling the soil and for companionship: "How much more agreeably could two male friends, rather than a man and woman, enjoy companionship and conversation in a life shared together. . . . Consequently, I do not see in what sense the woman was made as a helper for the man if not for the sake of bearing children."[11] For Augustine, the female body expresses the sexual aspect of the human being because it was created for sexual service through procreation. Since Augustine's doctrine of original sin designates sexual intercourse as the means of the transmission of sin, procreation is necessarily tainted. Thus, since procreation is woman's only role, Karen Torjesen notes that "the burden of guilt imposed by sinful sexuality rested more heavily on woman than man."[12]

Augustine's association of female sexuality with sin can be understood in the larger context of classical Greek culture in which female sexuality had been considered shameful and dangerous. According to Torjesen, "Female sexuality had to be controlled, because it represented danger and a threat to the male public order. Out-of-control female sexuality was dishonorable and shameless."[13] Thus the virtues of "courage, justice, and self-mastery" were designated for men as essential to develop their control and their participation in the public order. In contrast, women gained virtue through "chastity, silence, and obedience."[14]

Torjesen describes how a woman's virtue or honor was her "shame" in both Greek and Roman society: "Shame, the defining quality of womanhood, was indicated by passivity, subordination, and seclusion in the household."[15] While men gained honor in the public sphere, honorable women were those who limited their activities to their assigned place in the private sphere, the home. The seclusion of wives is portrayed on vase paintings. As Torjesen explains, "In the iconography of vase paintings, marital relations were indicated by a half-open door, which signified entry into the women's quarters—an inner space that could be locked and sealed off from the public male world."[16]

These constructions of women's virtue and women's place illuminate how justification for violence against wives is embedded in the conceptions of ideal womanhood that have prevailed for centuries in Western civilization. The construction of ideal womanhood as silent and obedient reinforces the practice of wife beating by granting virtue to the wife who submits to her husband, regardless of her husband's violent behavior.[17] Furthermore, the seclusion of wives in the home as portrayed on classical Greek vase paintings suggests that the private sphere of the home can be "sealed off" from the public world. The privatization of the wife's activities as under the control of her husband has provided a basis for the reluctance of public law officials to intervene in instances of domestic violence. Only in recent years have laws begun to change to protect the life of a married woman within her home.[18]

Women, the Image of God, and Violence against Wives

Augustine's theological association of female sexuality with sin reinforced the Greek view of women's sexuality as shameless and dangerous, and these views could be used to justify the husband's use of violence to control his wife. There is also a connection between support for wife beating and Augustine's resolution of another concern in the fifth-century Christian communities: Are women in the image of God?

Augustine's answer is found in his theory of the two-part soul based on Plato's association of male/soul and female/body, and on Augustine's own analogy of male and female in one flesh (Gen. 2:24). Augustine used these ideas to postulate two types of reason together in one soul. He associated the lower part of the soul with the female, and the higher part with the male who alone bears the image of God. However, since women who have been baptized have "clothed" themselves with Christ so there is "no longer male nor female" (Gal. 3:27–28), Augustine determined that women are in the image of God in the male, or higher reason, part of their souls.[19] A Christian woman can image God in the male part of her soul because her association with Christ overcomes her inferior female nature.

Augustine drew on this theory of the gendered soul to refute other leaders in the Christian communities who asserted—based on 1 Corinthians 11:7—that women were not in the image of God.[20] This verse provides an injunction for women to cover their heads because women are "the reflection of man," while men are "the image and reflection of God." As noted in chapter 2, Augustine resolved the conflict between this verse and Genesis 1:27 (male and female created in the image of God) by declaring that Genesis 1:27 refers to male and female *together* as one nature. Just as Augustine had used Genesis 2:24 (husband and wife become one flesh) to explain how higher and lower reason are together as male and female in one soul, he also used Genesis 2:24 to interpret Genesis 1:27. Therefore, "the woman together with her own husband is the image of God."[21]

However, when the woman is considered separately as "helper" (lower reason), she is not in the image of God.[22] A woman should cover her head because her female body represents the female, or lower, part of the soul; that is, woman does not bear the image of God in her body. As explained above, the image of God is only in the male, or higher, part of woman's soul. Furthermore, the covering indicates that female/lower reason "ought to be restrained" by the male/ higher reason because it is "dangerous" to lower reason to become too involved in temporal matters.[23] And when the female/lower reason "slips on too far by over-much progress into outward things," it is because the "masculine part which presides in the watch-tower of counsel [is] not restraining or bridling it."[24]

Augustine's image of how the male/higher reason should restrain and bridle the female/lower reason bears a frightening resemblance to the experience of one contemporary woman abused by her husband:

> My husband doesn't think I need to leave the house. He doesn't even let me go to church because he doesn't care to go. I can't belong to any clubs or organizations because my husband thinks a woman's place is in the home and no place else. . . . If I talk back to him, I end up with a busted mouth, a black eye, and bruises. I mentioned divorce once and he beat me up so bad I could hardly get out of bed for two days.[25]

This woman has been restrained and bridled to the point of being a prisoner in her own home.

Consistent with his view that female sexuality is sinful and female bodies do not bear the image of God, Augustine envisioned the relationship of a Christian husband to his wife as adversarial. He advised husbands to love their wives just as one should "love our enemies" (Matt. 5:44). Augustine explained, "In the same woman a good Christian loves the being that God has created, . . . while he *hates the corruptible and mortal relationship and marital intercourse.* In other words, it is evident that he loves her insofar as she is a human being, but that *he hates her under the aspect of wifehood*" (emphasis mine).[26]

It is a short step from this rhetoric of wife hating to the condoning of wife beating. This step is explicit in Augustine's praise of Monica, his own devout Christian mother. Augustine describes how Monica encouraged wives to submit to violence from their husbands because wives are bound by the marriage contract to serve their husbands as "masters."[27]

Augustine's rhetoric of wife hating and his praise of wives who submit to violent treatment from their husbands can be illuminated by analyzing his position in the context of the patristic church that declared asceticism to be the superior lifestyle for Christians. Rosemary Radford Ruether describes how the patristic elevation of virginity influenced the perception of the married Christian woman as a woman who had sunk "to the lowest position short of outright evil and become a 'mere wife.' "[28] In this lowest position of wife, "she is exhorted to be totally meek and to submit herself, mind and body," to the rule of her husband, who "has complete proprietary rights over her body, even to the point of physical abuse or death."[29] Ruether elaborates how this perception of the Christian wife "actually lowered the position of woman compared to more enlightened legislation in later Roman society as far as the *married woman* [Ruether's emphasis] was concerned."[30]

Thus, because they had lost their virginity, wives occupied the lowest rung in the spiritual hierarchy of the patristic church. Defiled by the very act of marital intercourse, married women became "the appropriate victims" of abuse within Christian families.[31] Given that wives are women who have chosen *not* to renounce the sinfulness of their bodies and their sexuality, they must suffer the consequences of being controlled by their husbands.

Early Modern Christianity: Martin Luther

The Protestant Reformation in the sixteenth century did not include a reformation of beliefs about the nature of woman or the subordination of wives to husbands.[32] Luther perpetuated the traditional beliefs that women are inferior by nature and responsible for original sin, and therefore women should be controlled by men as punishment for sin. The only changes to the traditional beliefs were the basis for judging women's inferiority and the method of control: women's nature was conceived as "weaker" rather than evil,[33] and with the closing of the convents, every woman was to become a wife subordinated under the rule of her husband.

Faith over Works and Husbands over Wives

Luther's argument for the subordination of wives to husbands is based on his adaptation of the traditional soul-over-body hierarchy. Luther follows Augustine in conceiving the soul as superior to the body, and thus the body should be controlled by the soul. However, by associating the soul with faith and the body with works, Luther adapts the traditional soul-over-body hierarchy to support his own argument for the primacy of faith over works. Furthermore, Luther does not follow Augustine in classifying parts of the soul with "higher reason" as male and "lower reason" as female. Luther dismisses this two-part soul theory as "unlearned and scholastic arguments."[34] Luther images the soul as a bride who is joined by the "wedding ring of faith" with Christ the bridegroom.[35] However, Luther's construct of the soul as feminine functions to continue the traditional devaluing of female by imaging the bride as a harlot: "Here this rich and divine bridegroom Christ marries this poor, wicked harlot, redeems her from all her evil, and adorns her with all his goodness."[36] The theory of the bridegroom as superior to the bride—and therefore the husband as superior to the wife—remains intact.

Although Luther does not agree with Augustine in assigning gender to parts of the soul, Luther does follow Augustine in associating wives with sin. Yet rather than associating female sexuality with sin, Luther's association of wives with sin is based on the analogy of husbands ruling over wives as faith should rule over sin.[37] In his diatribe against the Roman Catholic understanding of penance, Luther describes how faith should rule over the sinful conscience, a rule that employs violence: "Such faith, intent on the immutable truth of God, makes the conscience tremble, terrifies it and bruises it; and afterwards, when it is contrite, raises it up, consoles it, and preserves it."[38]

Luther's imagery of how faith rules over sin by inflicting terror and bruises closely resembles the behavioral pattern of husbands who physically abuse their wives. For example, Lenore E. Walker has identified three phases in the behavior of husbands who batter their wives: "the tension-building phase; the explosion or acute battering incident; and the calm, loving respite."[39] The second two phases that Walker identifies, "explosion" and "loving respite," parallel the "bruises" and "consoles" pattern that Luther describes.

As we seek to develop images of faith and sin that would support marital relationships of mutual empowerment, imagery such as Luther's in which faith can be associated with the violent behavior of husbands is not helpful. In the next chapter, I discuss Marjorie Suchocki's concept of sin as "unnecessary violence." The association of sin with violence, rather than the association of sin with wives who do not submit to their husbands, is useful in developing a theology of marriage that repudiates violence and enables mutual empowerment.

Women's Weaker Nature

Luther's reasoning for why wives should submit to husbands follows Augustine in portraying woman as inherently inferior in her capacity to reflect the image of God. Speaking of Eve in his commentary on Genesis 1:27, Luther writes that she "appears to be a somewhat different being from the man, having different members and a much weaker nature. Although she was a most extraordinary creature similar to Adam as far as the image of God is concerned, . . . she nevertheless was not equal of the male in glory and prestige."[40] Although there is no such inequality between female and male in the text of Genesis 1:27, Luther continues the tradition of interpreting Genesis 3:1 (Satan's question to Eve) as "proof" of woman's natural inferiority to man: "Satan's cleverness is perceived also in this, that he attacks the weak part of the human nature, Eve the woman, not Adam the man. . . . I, too, believe that if he had tempted Adam first, the victory would have been Adam's."[41]

Eve is held responsible for human sin due to her weaker nature, which Satan recognized,[42] and in his commentary on Genesis 3:16 (the husband shall rule over his wife), Luther names the husband's rule as "punishment [that] is inflicted on the woman." Furthermore, similar to how Augustine describes his mother, Monica, encouraging wives to accept violent treatment from their husbands, Luther imagines Eve "giving comfort to Adam" with these words: "I have sinned. . . . Therefore we women should bear the hardship and wretchedness of conceiving, of giving birth, and of obeying you husbands."[43] Luther provides additional theological legitimation for the submission of wives to husbands by drawing a parallel between God and husbands. After taking their marriage vows, wives are admonished to "submit yourselves unto your own husbands, as unto the Lord," following the command of Ephesians 5:22.[44]

As further "punishment" for Eve's sin, Luther believes that women are deprived of even the ability to act in the public sphere. Although the location of the wife's subordination is not specified in Genesis 3:16, Luther argues that women are to stay home:

> This punishment, too, springs from original sin. . . . The rule remains with the husband and the wife is compelled to obey him by God's command. He rules the home and the state, wages wars, defends his possessions, tills the soil, builds, plants, etc. The woman, on the other hand, is like a nail driven into the wall. She sits at home. . . . So the wife should stay at home and look after the affairs of the household, as one who has been deprived of the ability of administering those affairs that are outside and that concern the state.[45]

Luther describes the rule of the husband as operative in both the public and private spheres.[46] Consistent with his insistence on the complete rule of the husband, Luther denigrates the rule of women in home and state in his commentary on Ecclesiastes 7:26. A woman who "assumes authority over her husband" engages in a work that "comes from her own fault and from evil" because she was not "created" for this work.[47] Expanding the subordination of wives to include all women, Luther assumes that when a woman "is put into the place of the king . . . she always has a senate of leading men, by whose counsel everything should be administered."[48] In his commentary on Ecclesiastes 7:28,

Luther writes that "not even one" woman is "fit to rule . . . and this is because of a divine ordinance."[49] In an argument with Katherine von Bora, his own wife, Luther declares:

> I concede to you the control of the household, provided my rights are preserved. Female government has never done any good. God made Adam master over all creatures, to rule over all living things, but when Eve persuaded him that he was lord even over God she spoiled everything. We have you women to thank for that! With tricks and cunning women deceive men, as I, too, have experienced.[50]

In contrast to Augustine, who argues that women's bodies evidence women's sinfulness, Luther believes women's physical and mental characteristics reveal that women are created to stay home and under their husbands' rule. Luther grants that women "certainly have the words" to talk about politics, "yet they do not grasp and talk about the matter in hand. This is why they speak so confusedly and absurdly when they talk about politics that nothing could be worse."[51] Assuming that the bodies of all women and men conform to one particular shape, Luther proclaims that men's broad shoulders and narrow hips indicate their intelligence. In contrast, women's narrow shoulders and broad hips indicate they should stay home because they have "a wide fundament to sit upon."[52]

In Luther's imagination, not only does the shape of woman's body indicate she should stay home, but through her role as wife a woman is the home, or "building of God." In his commentary on Genesis 2:22, Luther describes this building as a source of joy for husbands:

> Not only is the house built through them [wives] by
> procreation and other services that are necessary in
> a household; but the husbands themselves are built
> through them, because wives are, as it were, a nest and
> dwelling place where husbands can go to spend their
> time and dwell with joy.[53]

Here Luther's contention that husbands can find joy with
their wives is in contrast to his view that women use "tricks
and cunning" to deceive men (as quoted above). Perhaps
one explanation for this ambiguity in Luther's writings was
that the traditional beliefs about women were at odds with
the behavior of actual women in Luther's time.

Similar to Augustine's theological justification for
women's subordination at a time—in the fourth and fifth
centuries—when women had been refusing subordination, Luther's assertion that women do not have the ability to administer affairs outside the home is pronounced
at a time when women of both the upper class and working class had been active in the public sphere. During the
medieval period, upper-class women had been exercising
considerable administrative authority in both secular society and the church. For example, the land-based feudal system depended on women of the nobility to manage and
defend their land in the absence of their husbands.[54] In the
medieval church, women organized and ruled convents, a
rule that also included management of land. And one of
these women, Hildegard of Bingen (1098–1179), who was
an abbess in the Rhineland valley of Germany, emerged as
an international political advisor.[55] The behavior of women
such as Hildegard was intolerable in Luther's construction
of woman as wife. As Lyndal Roper notes, "The very idea

that women might hold positions of power could be viewed as unchristian, contrary to the right order of subjugation which ought to exist between women and men."[56]

Luther's metaphor of the wife sitting at home "like a nail driven into the wall" was also not applicable to women of the working classes during the Middle Ages. In addition to working as an individual in her own business or as her husband's assistant in his trade,[57] some working-class women also acted collectively in the public sphere. For example, in 1455 the "silk women" of London petitioned Parliament to ask the king to order an embargo on all finished silk entering England "from beyond the sea."[58] The women's petition was granted with the exception of girdles from Genoa.

Even Luther's own wife, Katherine von Bora, did not sit at home. Her activities included the following, both inside and beyond her home:

> Katie looked after an orchard beyond the village, which supplied them with apples, grapes, pears, nuts, and peaches. She had also a fish pond from which she netted trout, carp, pike, and perch. She looked after the barnyard with hens, ducks, pigs, and cows, and did the slaughtering herself. . . . In later years he [Luther] acquired a farm at Zulsdorf, which Katie managed, spending there some weeks out of the year. Luther wrote to her on such occasions: . . . "To my beloved wife, Katherine, Mrs. Dr. Luther, mistress of the pig market, lady of Zulsdorf, and whatsoever other titles may befit thy Grace."[59]

Luther's construction of the wife sitting at home was inconsistent with the lives of actual women. However, his construction of the subordination of wives to husbands as "punishment" did provide theological justification from a Protestant perspective for existing church and civil laws that permitted husbands, both clergy and lay, to beat their wives.[60] In the *Decretum*, the canon law compiled by Gratian in the twelfth century, the husband's chastisement of his wife should not include beating her. However, a century later in his theological encyclopedia, the Dominican Nicolas Byard interpreted the chastisement named in the *Decretum* as including beating "for her correction," but not whipping her as a master was permitted to whip a slave.[61]

Documents and woodcuts from the later medieval period portray the treatment of wives according to civil and customary laws. In contrast to canon law that forbade whipping, the common law "Rule of Thumb" allowed a man to "whip his wife provided that he use a switch no thicker than his thumb."[62] However, a German manuscript of 1456 includes a woodcut that portrays a husband hitting his wife, who is on her knees, with a club much wider than his thumb.[63] The most popular manual of duties for upper-class society in the fourteenth century was the *Book of the Knight of La Tour-Landry* (of the Tower). It was published in eight editions before 1538 in French, English, and German. In it, the Knight tells his daughters how one husband broke his wife's nose because she dared to rebuke him in public.[64] This wife got what she deserved for her insubordinate behavior. Even worse, she was insubordinate in public, the sphere in which she had no authority.[65] In addition to these formal documents, common sayings of the period reveal an attitude that encouraged violence toward women. For example, "A woman, spaniel and a walnut tree, the more they are beaten, better they be."[66]

Luther's Ambiguity on Wife Beating

In 1532 Luther offered an alternative to the church and civil laws with his vision for Christian marital relations in his sermon on 1 Peter 3:1–6. Wives will be "obedient and submissive," and husbands will refrain from "blows" regardless of their spouse's behavior. To the husbands, Luther declares: "For you will accomplish nothing with blows; they will not make a woman pious and submissive. If you beat one devil out of her, you will beat two into her."[67] Luther acknowledges the magnitude of violence between husbands and wives as he laments that "everyone" follows the secular laws: "But no one enjoys doing what God has commanded. On the other hand, everybody hastens to do what men have invented."[68] In another sermon, Luther appealed to woman's "weaker" nature as cause for husbands to sometimes "overlook" their wives' behavior and "indulge her with a kind word," even though this behavior contradicts popular opinion;[69] husbands who did not beat their wives to enforce the husband's rule were subject to public ridicule.[70]

However, in his commentary on 1 Corinthians 7:27–28, Luther also appeals to woman's nature as "weak and fragile" to explain why "one seldom finds a good marriage where love and peace are at home." He also observes in this commentary that because "God made woman subject to man, . . . her spirit must be broken often."[71] Luther uses adversarial imagery when he, like Augustine, applies the symbol of "enemy" to wives. Yet whereas Augustine admonishes the Christian husband to "hate in her [his wife] the corruptible and mortal conjugal connection," Luther's enemy is the disobedient wife. "If wives are disobedient, self-willed, and domineering," writes Luther, "a man hates his own home and feels as if he is going to war and entering the enemies' camp when he steps into his house."[72]

Yet God expects husbands to treat their wives "considerately"; this enemy is to be "helped" rather than "harmed." "God leaves it to everyone to treat his wife considerately according to each wife's nature," writes Luther. "You must not use your authority arbitrarily; for you are her husband to help, support, and protect her, not to harm her. . . . Here you yourself must know how to proceed thoughtfully."[73] However, Luther's appeal to knowledge or reason as the husband's guide is problematic given Luther's theological treatment of reason. Luther argued, against the medieval scholastics, that human reason is completely corrupted by sin so that reason is "blind and ignorant," and humans cannot even know the good.[74]

Thus Luther's attitude toward corporal chastisement of wives is ambiguous. As stated above, Luther preached that husbands should use "kind words" rather than "blows."[75] Yet according to the recorders of *Table Talk*, he did not always practice what he preached in his treatment of Katherine von Bora, his own wife. Luther is quoted as saying, "Whenever Katie gets saucy, she gets nothing but a box on the ear."[76] On another occasion, Luther defined domestic violence in this way: "Domestic wrath is our Lord God's plaything; there only a slap or a cuff applies."[77] In comparison to secular laws of the day that permitted a man to beat his wife with a stick, these statements could be interpreted as sympathetic to wives, condoning *only* "a box on the ear" or a "slap or a cuff." Yet such statements function to support the belief that violence is permissible in order to control a wife's behavior, to "break her spirit," to enforce her subordination to her husband.

Luther's perpetuation of the traditional subordination of wives to husbands as the ideal for Christian couples conflicts with his premise of the "priesthood of all believers," a premise that provides a theological basis for offering freedom and equality to men *and* women.[78] Yet this premise was not actualized in practice even though Luther specifically named wives and husbands in his argument that "all Christians" are priests.[79] Similar to Augustine's resolution of the conflict between Genesis 1:27 and Genesis 2:7—that women are spiritually equal to men but temporally subordinate[80]—Luther proclaimed, "For inwardly . . . there is no difference between a man and a woman. Externally, however, God wants the husband to rule and the wife to be submissive to him."[81]

Thus Luther's new theology of marriage that mitigated the husband's use of violence still functioned to strengthen the old theology of the husband's rule.[82] Bonnie S. Anderson and Judith P. Zinsser name how the subordination of wives united men across the religious divide of this period. They write, "For the learned Catholic and Protestant churchmen of the sixteenth and seventeenth century, marriage meant . . . the traditional relationship between women and men was the way to keep women subordinate and obedient."[83] For centuries, the societal structure of marital relationships had been reinforced from a Christian perspective by an emphasis on Genesis 3:16 (the husband's rule over his wife). Luther continued this traditional emphasis even though it conflicted with his nontraditional theology of the laity as the "priesthood of all believers."[84] While he dismantled the hierarchical Roman Catholic priesthood, he upheld the traditional hierarchy of husband over wife. Within this marital hierarchy in a society that gave legal sanction to husbands who beat their wives, Luther did the best he could by admonishing Christian husbands to treat their wives with reason and consideration.

Foundations for the Contemporary Period: Sigmund Freud

Freud's view of religion and its impact on humanity can be summed up in the title of his book *The Future of an Illusion.* The illusion is religion, and its future is to be discarded for human rationality so that civilization can progress toward maturity.[85] Yet with few exceptions, Freud's theories function to support traditional Christian ideas about the body, sin, sexuality, and women. This support is evident in the images Freud uses in describing the psychical processes of the mind and in the way Freud reinforces the connection between sexual desire and sin with his theory of the primal horde. Furthermore, his theories about psychosexual development reinforce the notion of women's physical and moral inferiority. These theories provide psychological justification for the practice of wife beating as well as for his rebuking of his female contemporaries who were challenging women's subordination.

The Mind and Gender

Similar to the gendering of the soul by Augustine and Luther, Freud assigned gender in his descriptions of the psychical processes of the mind.[86] Freud associated the functioning of the super-ego with the father: "The super-ego retains the character of the father," and "The super-ego arises, as we know, from an identification with the father taken as a model."[87] Freud also attributed maleness to the ego when he wrote that "hidden behind the ego's dread of the super-ego, the fear of conscience," is "probably" the "dread of castration."[88]

In contrast to the masculinity of the super-ego and the ego, Freud implied an association of the id with femininity. Freud described the id as the "dark, inaccessible part of our personality; . . . a chaos, a cauldron full of seething excitations."[89] Similarly, Freud described female sexuality as a "dark continent,"[90] "veiled in impenetrable obscurity,"[91] and he referred to the nature of femininity as a "riddle."[92] Freud also associated women with the id when he postulated that women have "less capacity" than men for "sublimating their instincts"[93] because both women and the id are characterized by a connection with instincts. As Susan Griffin notes, "In Freud's vision of the id, we find the same apocryphal flavor which exists in the image of the witch, the femme fatale, and the female vampire of the nineteenth century."[94]

Furthermore, both the id and females are morally deficient. Freud wrote that the id "knows no judgments of value: no good and evil, no morality."[95] Similarly, females are biologically determined to remain morally immature because a girl lacks the fear of castration necessary to resolve her Oedipus complex (her desire for her father), and thus the development of her super-ego is arrested. "[In girls,] the formation of the super-ego must suffer; it cannot attain the strength and independence which give it its cultural significance, and feminists are not pleased when we point out to them the effects of this factor upon the average feminine character."[96]

Freud maintained the traditional subordination of women to men with his association of the id with the female and the ego with the male because the function of the ego is to control the id. The association of the id with the feminine also upholds the traditional identification of women with the body, as the id is the psychical process most closely associated with the body.

Original Sin and Sexual Desire

Freud also maintained the traditional association of sin with sexuality. Although their definition of sin is different, both Augustine and Freud posited the origin of sin in desire. In Augustine's doctrine of original sin, the root of sin is pride, because Adam and Eve desired to be like God.[97] In postulating the origin of human relationships, Freud replaced the story of the fall of Adam and Eve with his theory of the primal horde. Freud named original sin as the murder of the primal father by his sons because the sons sexually desired their mother and sisters.[98]

Freud's theory of original sin functions to strengthen the traditional connection between sin and sexual desire.[99] Whereas Augustine declared that uncontrolled sexual desire was the *penalty* for the original sin of pride, Freud named sexual desire as the *origin* or "chief motive" for the original sin of murder. Freud believed that the Christian doctrine of atonement substantiated his theory of original sin as the murder of the father: "If, however, Christ redeemed mankind from the burden of original sin by the sacrifice of his own life, we are driven to conclude that the sin was a murder. . . . And if this sacrifice of a life brought about atonement with God the Father, the crime to be expiated can only have been the murder of the father."[100]

Yet in contrast to Augustine, who designates the physical act of sexual intercourse as the means of inheritance, Freud believes that inheritance occurs through the psychical processes of the mind. He explains, "[In] the id, which is capable of being inherited, are harboured residues of the existences of countless egos; and, when the ego forms its super-ego out of the id, it may perhaps only be reviving shapes of former egos and be bringing them to resurrection."[101] Thus while Freud's theory reinforces the traditional connection between sin and sexual desire, his theory differs from the traditional naming of the body as the carrier of sin.

Finally, both Augustine and Freud posit original sin as a rebellion against the Father to gain what the Father has. Adam and Eve revolt against the heavenly Father to gain the knowledge of good and evil; the brothers murder their earthly father to gain sexual rights to their mother and sisters. However, the role of women in these rebellions is quite different. In contrast to Eve, who thinks and acts for herself, the females of the primal horde are passive. Relegated to the role of objects of desire, these females function only as the "chief motive" for the males committing the murder. They do not participate in the murder nor in the "beginnings of morality and law"—that is, the institution of the laws against incest and murder instigated by the brothers after they murder their father.[102]

Women's Innate Inferiority, Masochism, and Moral Agency

In the scenes of Freud's primal horde drama, the girls and women are hardly on the stage. Consistent with their silence and absence from the "beginnings of morality and law," Freud constructs a psychology of women that explains why women are inferior and incapable of developing the moral agency necessary to act in the public sphere.

According to Freud, the basis for the girl to feel that her body is inferior is her lack of a penis.[103] Following Luther, who asserted that women have "different members and a much weaker nature," Freud creates a hierarchy out of the "different members." The penis is the norm, and the clitoris is the deviation: "The only bodily organ which is really regarded as inferior is the atrophied penis, a girl's clitoris."[104]

For Freud, women's possession of a clitoris rather than a penis is not only a biological fact; it is also the basis for devaluing women: "As a result of the discovery of women's lack of a penis they [women] are debased in value for girls just as they [women] are for boys and later perhaps for men."[105] Freud's construction of female bodies (and therefore women) as inferior and less valuable than male bodies (and therefore men) supports the belief that men should control women because the superior should control the inferior. As Jane Flax observes, "The child recognizes not just difference in bodies but a social hierarchy."[106]

Freud describes the girl's reaction to the sight of the penis: "She makes her judgment and her decision in a flash. She has seen it and knows she is without it and wants to have it."[107] Similar to Augustine, who cannot imagine an identity for woman other than in relation to man as a "helper" for procreation, Freud's statement implies that a girl's sexual identity is formed in relation to a boy as expressed by her desire for his penis.

The boy's reaction to the discovery of sexual difference is quite different from the girl's response. Freud suggests that the "sight of a girl's genital region" elicits reactions of either "horror of the mutilated creature or triumphant contempt for her," and these reactions *permanently* determine the boy's relations to women" (emphasis mine).[108] Here Freud creates a psychological basis for male violence against females as males may choose to express their horror and contempt through violence.

Freud also provides psychological justification for why females would submit to male violence with his association of femininity with masochism. Based on his theory of the suppression of female aggression, Freud explains why masochism is feminine: "The suppression of women's aggressiveness which is prescribed for them constitutionally and imposed on them socially favours the development of powerful masochistic impulses, which succeed, as we know, in binding erotically the destructive trends which have been diverted inwards. Thus masochism, as people say, is truly feminine."[109]

Furthermore, Freud discusses the association of beating with love. Freud explains why some of his female clients became sexually aroused by creating fantasies of being beaten by their father:

> 'My father loves me' was meant in a genital sense; owing to the regression it is turned into 'My father is beating me (I am being beaten by my father)'. This being beaten is now a convergence of the sense of guilt and sexual love. *It is not only the punishment for the forbidden genital relation, but also the regressive substitute for that relation* [Freud's emphasis]. . . . Here for the first time we have the essence of masochism.[110]

Here Freud invokes his theory of the Oedipal complex in the relationship between a girl and her father to explain how a woman could conflate beating with sexual love. In time the girl should replace her father with her husband, and if her husband beats her, she may believe the beating is a demonstration of love.

Freud logically follows his association of femininity with masochism by associating masculinity with sadism. Freud postulates that sadism has its "roots in male aggressiveness," and he does not consider it a "perversion" for a male to have an "active or *violent attitude* toward the sexual object" (emphasis mine).[111] Here Freud takes the fact of male violence toward a sexual partner and labels this violence as not perverted or as normal.

Freud's theories of masochism as feminine and sadism as masculine offer psychological justification for male violence against females. These theories have two particularly negative consequences for relationships between women and men: first, the assertion that females are inferior to males supports the notion that the superior should control the inferior; and second, the use of the Oedipus complex suggests that women can equate love with beating. As Rosemary Radford Ruether has argued, "Psychoanalysis has become the chief tool, replacing patriarchal religion, for rationalizing and sanctifying the inferiority of women."[112]

In addition to explaining why females are physically inferior and masochistic, Freud's construction of female psychological development postulates females as incapable of mature moral development. Not incidentally, Freud's "scientific" constructions of femininity supported traditional Christian ideas about women's inferior nature and need to be subordinate at a time when the authority of the Western Christian church was being questioned. For example, the church was confronted by controversies with Charles Darwin and the developing scientific movement, as well as challenges from theologians and philosophers such as Ludwig Feuerbach and Karl Marx.

The larger cultural context for the reception of Freud's theories about women also included challenges by actual women to the traditional ideal of womanhood. As discussed above, Augustine's exegesis of biblical texts was in response to women refusing submission to men in the fourth and fifth centuries, and Luther's construction of the ideal wife staying at home was in tension with the activities of real women in the late medieval period. Similarly, Freud developed his theories at the end of the 1800s and the early 1900s, a time when some women had been refusing restriction to the private sphere of the home. Throughout the 1800s these women had assumed their responsibility as moral agents in the public sphere to work for social reform, including suffrage and legal sanctions against husbands who physically abused their wives.[113] And "The Women's Charter of Rights and Liberties" of 1909 included a section that specifically addressed violence against women.[114]

By entering the public sphere and asserting themselves as moral agents, women were creating an alternative to the traditional dichotomy of woman as "good" wife at home or "bad" prostitute in public. Women in Freud's own country of Austria were at the forefront of this movement.[115] For example, Bertha Pappenheim, the "Anna O" of Josef Breuer's and Freud's famous case of hysteria, became a social worker and an activist for women's rights after her creation of the "talking cure" with Breuer. She was also a long-standing friend of Martha Freud, Sigmund's wife.[116] Moving to Frankfurt, Pappenheim raised the funds necessary to found an institution to care for girls who were delinquent or retarded, and for pregnant, unwed girls and their babies. In addition, she translated *A Vindication of the Rights of Women* by Mary Wollstonecraft (published in 1792) from English into German, and paid to have it printed.[117] These examples of women acting in the public sphere create a picture of women refusing to be limited to traditional roles as they claimed moral agency and control of their bodies from sexual and economic exploitation.

In contrast to the behavior of actual women, Freud elaborated his conception of the Oedipus complex to construct a theoretical woman hardly capable of moral action. To develop this theory, Freud used the physical differences between males and females. When a boy discovers that girls do not have a penis, he fears he will lose his penis; he fears being castrated by his father as punishment for the boy's desire for his mother. The fear generated by this "castration complex" is sufficient to drive the boy from his mother and enable him to identify with his father. Thus the boy resolves his Oedipus complex, which leads to the creation of his super-ego or moral agency.

However, when a girl discovers she does not have a penis, she is filled with a sense of inferiority, an envy of the boy's penis, and a desire for her father because he has a penis. The young girl, having no penis, cannot fear castration and thus she has great difficulty in overcoming her Oedipus complex. Freud explains, "Girls remain in it for an indeterminate length of time; they demolish it late and, even so, incompletely. In these circumstances the formation of the super-ego must suffer."[118]

Not only does a female's lack of a penis inhibit her moral development, her envious desire for a penis also impairs her ability to act with justice in the social sphere.

> The fact that women must be regarded as having little sense of justice is no doubt related to the predominance of envy in their mental life; for the demand for justice is a modification of envy and lays down the condition subject to which one can put envy aside. We also regard women as weaker in their social interests and as having less capacity for sublimating their instincts than men.[119]

Freud's assertion that women have "little sense of justice" is in stark contrast to the behavior of women who had been demanding justice in the decades before Freud published his theory of women's moral inferiority to men. With this construction of feminine character, Freud provides psychological "verification" for the traditional theological conception that women are innately morally inferior to men. Whereas Luther attributes female weakness to their nature as created by God, Freud constructs this weakness as an arrested development of the super-ego.

Both Luther and Freud use physical characteristics as the basis for their construction of woman's role as limited to the home. Luther determines that women "ought to stay home" because "women have narrow shoulders and broad hips"; Freud believes women's lack of a penis renders them incapable of developing the morality necessary to act in the public sphere. These theories based on physical characteristics of women have been used to justify the physical restriction of women to the home, and this restriction has implications for creating the conditions for violence against wives. Emerson and Russell Dobash, in their work entitled *Violence against Wives*, name how the restriction of wives to the home deprives them of a social life. As the husband gains increasing control over his wife's activities, the conditions for domestic violence are created.[120] Thus for some women who become wives, their restriction to the home—a restriction supported by Freud's theory of women's incapability for mature moral development—causes them great pain and suffering.

Rather than describing actual moral inferiority of women, Freud's Oedipal theory of arrested moral development functions to portray how a female remained in a perpetual legal state of childhood and immaturity.[121] For example, until women won the right to vote in the twentieth century, wives had the same status as young children before the law.[122] Barbara Corrado Pope notes how the law in the nineteenth century "particularly oppressed married women. They were treated either as civilly non-existent for most of the century (in English common law) or as minors (according to the Napoleonic Code). They had no political rights, almost no economic power, and little judicial recourse in case of *maltreatment* or the infidelity of their husbands" (emphasis mine).[123] In the years following her invention of the "talking cure" with Breuer and Freud, Bertha Pappenheim expressed frustration with the lack of legal justice for women: "If there will be justice in the world to come, women will be law-givers and men will have to have babies."[124] Justice was slow indeed for wives who were recipients of their husbands' violence. Not until the closing decade of the twentieth century has the law been changed so that evidence concerning the abuse suffered by an abused woman is admissible at her trial if she killed her abuser.[125]

In addition to having virtually no legal rights, the women who were Freud's contemporaries were also trivialized and ridiculed for their social reform efforts by some of the publications of the day.[126] Thus Freud's construction of women's inferior moral development can be understood as a negative reaction or backlash against the public moral action of women in the nineteenth century.[127]

Women's Inferior, Sinful Nature and Violence against Wives

To summarize: Augustine's writings offer a theological justification for the belief in the innate inferiority of female nature to male nature, and thus the necessity for women to be controlled by men. Augustine uses this rationale for the control of women as a basis for admonishing Christian wives to submit to the control of their husbands, even if this control includes physical abuse. Augustine praises his own mother, Monica, both for submitting to violence from her husband and for encouraging other wives to do the same.

Building on the Greek philosophical hierarchy of the superior male soul over the inferior female body and the Greco-Roman legal concepts of woman's weaker nature and dangerous sexuality, Augustine interprets biblical texts to justify the subordination of women to men from a Christian perspective. He interprets the creation of Adam in Genesis

2:7 to prove that women are inferior to men because the first woman was created after the first man. Augustine also establishes woman's "natural" inferiority to man by associating women and sin with the body and sexuality. Following his designation of sexual intercourse as the means of the transmission of original sin, wives are particularly tainted with sin due to their role in procreation. Augustine's interpretation of Eve's creation as "helper" (Gen. 2:18) reinforces the association of wives with the inferior body and sinful procreation because Augustine cannot imagine that a woman could help a man in any way other than in procreation. Thus he concludes that procreation is the sole purpose for the creation of women. As mentioned earlier, with these beliefs about the sinful nature of women's bodies and sexuality, Augustine suggests an adversarial marital relationship. He advises Christian husbands to love their wives as Christians are to love their enemies, and to "hate" in their wives the wife's role in sexual intercourse. This theological rhetoric of wife hating can be conducive to legitimating the cultural practice of wife beating.

Furthermore, woman's inferior nature is set forth in Augustine's theory of a gendered two-part soul. According to this theory, the female body does not bear the image of God; in women, the image of God is found only in the higher, male part of their souls. Therefore, a woman is in the image of God *only* when considered together with her own husband. Because women alone are not in the image of God, they should be "restrained" by men; this restraint is symbolized by women covering their heads. Thus the subordination of women to men is the proper model for correct Christian behavior. And in the case of sinful wives, violence perpetrated by husbands is permissible in order to maintain subordination.

Although Luther describes women's nature as "weak" rather than evil, he uses this conception of weakness to perpetuate the traditional beliefs that women are inherently inferior by nature and responsible for original sin. Thus wives should be subordinate to their husbands as punishment for Eve's sin. Just as faith should rule over sin, husbands should rule over wives. Luther reinforces this construction of sinful wives and faithful husbands with his imagery of the soul as a bride joined in marriage to Christ: the bride is a "wicked harlot." Luther's use of punishment as the basis for the subordination of wives to husbands provides theological justification from a Protestant perspective for canon and civil laws that permitted husbands to chastise their wives with physical abuse.

Luther's theology of marriage functions to tighten the system of male control as every woman is to become a wife who stays home under the rule of her husband. Following his belief that the husband's rule is based in punishment, Luther observes that the wife's "spirit must be broken often," and if the wife is disobedient, Luther refers to the home as "the enemies' camp." Luther defines domestic violence as "our Lord God's plaything; there only a slap or cuff applies," and his own wife, Katie, received "nothing but a box on the ear."

In addition to these explicit examples of condoning the husband's use of violence, Luther's theology also implicitly undergirds violence against wives, for his description of how faith should rule the sinful conscience parallels the behavior of husbands who beat their wives. Thus, although Luther admonished husbands *not* to beat their wives, his theoretical construction of woman's nature and subordination as a wife functions to support a husband who uses violence to enforce his rule over his wife, a rule conceived as punishment for sin.

Freud's theories provide psychological justification to reinforce the theological conception of the innate inferiority of woman's nature. Following Augustine, Luther believed woman to be deficient in her ability to image God; Freud also constructed woman as deficient: she lacks a penis. In the nineteenth century, when the authority of the Christian church was challenged by the discoveries of the scientific revolution, Freud's theories of women's psychosexual development functioned to provide "scientific" justification for the traditional subjugation of women to men, a subjugation that provides the context for violence against wives.

The subjugation of wives to husbands is exacerbated by the traditional restriction of wives to the home, where the wife is economically and sexually dependent on her husband. As the husband assumes more and more control of his wife's activities, the wife is susceptible to violence from her husband if she questions his control. In support of the wife's restriction to the private sphere of the home, both Luther and Freud argue for woman's inability to act in the public sphere. Luther attributes this inability as punishment for the sin of Eve, while Freud uses his Oedipal theory to explain why women are unable to develop the moral maturity necessary to be concerned about issues of social justice.

Furthermore, Freud associates masculinity with sadism and femininity with masochism in his construction of psychosexual development. He utilizes these associations to explain why a man's attitude of violence toward a sexual partner is normal, and how a woman can equate love with beating. Thus Freud's theories provide psychological justification for husbands who beat their wives and wives who stay with their abusive husbands.

In this chapter I have analyzed how Augustine, Luther, and Freud utilized their understandings of body, soul, sin, and sexuality to construct theories that proved the innate physical and moral inferiority of women. Due to this inferiority, wives should be subordinate to husbands, and the husband's use of some form of violence is permissible to enforce this subordination. In the next two chapters, I develop alternative Christian theories of sin, body, soul, and sexuality that do not denigrate women—theories that could function to create mutually empowering relationships between wives and husbands.

CHAPTER FOUR

Rethinking Sin

I thank God for letting me still have Buddy [my child]. And I remembered having the same reaction after Frank [my husband] would beat me, thanking the Lord for giving me the strength to take it. And I remembered thanking the Lord for each day that my mother lived even when she was spitting up blood and praying for me to kill her. I looked in my mother's eyes pleading for me to help her, and all I could do was pray. While you were gone, I was holding Buddy, and I thought if that bastard Frank Bennett ever tries to take my child, I won't pray. I'll break his neck.

Fried Green Tomatoes[1]

This scene from the film *Fried Green Tomatoes* could be viewed as a woman rethinking her definition of sin. The behavior she once believed to be good, she now considers sinful because she did not act sooner to remove herself and her child from her husband's violence, nor did she act to relieve her mother's suffering. While this chapter does *not* advocate that wives respond with violence to their husbands' actions or make an argument for euthanasia, this chapter does propose that some beliefs deemed as good are actually sin, and vice versa. For example, in marriage, the subordination of the wife that was considered good is actually sin.

Sin is a violation of the interrelatedness of all creation, a disruption of relationships that causes harm to oneself or to another. God has created us to develop and thrive in a community of positive relationships; therefore, causing harm is sin because we are rejecting the best possibility offered to us by God in each moment that could lead toward redemption. Thus, while a relational world offers opportunities for enrichment, these relationships also increase our vulnerability to sin. Our very becoming can be enhanced or diminished by our interactions with each other. Because we are constituted by our relationships in a relational world, intimate partners have great power to actualize sin and redemption in their relationship with each other and with their community.

The traditional associations of sin with the body, sexuality, and women have been used to justify the traditional marriage model of dominant husband/submissive wife and the use of violence to maintain the wife's submission (as argued in chapter 3). This disciplinary model of marriage makes genuine intimacy and mutual empowerment between wives and husbands more difficult to achieve in Christian marriage. Alternative understandings of sin are needed because denigrating the body, sexuality, and women diminishes mutuality. Furthermore, the ordering of husbands over wives is the result of sin and thus should not be used as a model for

Christian marriage. Couples who practice relational power and mutuality offer a model more representative of God's intention for right relations.

Despite the widespread association of sin with women, the body, and sexuality, some Christian theologians have proposed alternative views. Friedrich Schleiermacher explains sin as whatever obstructs God-consciousness; Paul Tillich understands sin as estrangement from God, self, and others; and Marjorie Suchocki defines sin as unnecessary violence. The understandings of sin proposed by both Schleiermacher and Suchocki are based on the interrelatedness of all creation and describe how sin is transmitted or inherited without denigrating the body or sexuality. Tillich's work illuminates the anxiety of becoming a self by practicing relational power with an intimate partner or leaving a partner who is abusive, and he associates sexuality with the sacred. None of these theologians imagine that women are more responsible for sin or more likely to sin than men. By disassociating the definition of sin with the body, sexuality, and women, and by providing theological grounds for repudiating violence against wives, each of these theologians offers resources for developing a doctrine of sin that can enhance opportunities for redemption through intimacy in partner relationships.

Sin as Obstruction to God-Consciousness

Schleiermacher's understanding of sin is important for the new paradigm of marriage as mutual empowerment because he explains the universality of sin (without biblicism) in a way that frees women of the legacy of Eve, redeems sexuality, and squarely places sin in the corporate nature of human life. His understanding of the corporate nature of sin also provides a theological basis for explaining the pervasiveness of violence against wives.[2]

The Tendency for Self-Centeredness in Females and Males

In contrast to Augustine's designation of "pride" and Luther's naming of "unbelief" as the root of sin, Schleiermacher locates the cause of sin in the development of human consciousness. As humans develop through time, physicality precedes spirituality. In this initial physical stage, humans are only aware of themselves as individuals distinct from others; they are literally only "self-conscious." Other beings are perceived merely as coexisting in the same time and place.[3] During this stage of self-consciousness, the spirit is striving to "break through into consciousness," a striving that Schleiermacher describes as "an original and innate tendency of the human soul."[4] Eventually, spirit enters human consciousness. We become aware of our feeling of absolute dependence on God and of our connectedness to the whole of the universe.[5] Because the feeling of absolute dependence includes being in relation with all other beings as well as God, humans now have the ability to regard and respect others, to be concerned for the preservation of the whole in contrast to an earlier concern for the preservation of only the individual self.

The beginning of God-consciousness is the point at which we become truly human and capable of sin. We simultaneously realize both our consciousness of our relatedness to God and all creation, and our resistance to this consciousness of relatedness; this resistance is sin.[6] Because God-consciousness is our consciousness of our related-ness to God and all creation, sin applies only to things that obstruct the development of this consciousness.[7] Further-more, sin is virtually inevitable because we have the "habit" for self-centeredness in our physicality that emerged first in our evolution as human beings.[8] Due to the strength of this habit, we sin as we continue to be concerned only with self-preservation.[9] Thus the tendency to sin is a habit of our physicality that was established before we became fully human, and we sin when, after becoming fully human, we deny our interrelatedness to God and each other.

Therefore, Schleiermacher disagrees with the tradi-tional view that human nature was altered by the first sin because the tendency to sin is a characteristic of human nature. If human nature was changed by the first act of sin, then our identity as a species would not be the same as that of our first parents: "The terms 'individual' and 'spe-cies' lose their meaning unless everything met within the individual, whether successively or simultaneously, can be understood from and explained by the nature of the spe-cies."[10] The action of one individual could not alter an entire species because an individual can only act according to the characteristics of the species: "Still less is it possible to sup-pose that such an alteration of nature should have resulted from an act of the alleged individual as such, since the indi-vidual can act only *in accordance with* the nature of his spe-cies, but never can act *upon* that nature [Schleiermacher's emphasis]."[11]

Rather, the first humans sinned because they had the same inclination prior to the moment of sin as we do—that is, our habit or instinct for self-awareness is stronger than our consciousness of our relatedness to God and others. If human nature was not altered by the sin of the first pair of individuals, then the characteristic that supposedly developed after their sin must have been present before they sinned. When the first humans sinned, "they were simply the first-born of sinfulness"; their actions are not the reason for acts of sin by succeeding generations.[12] This view shifts the blame for sin from the actions of the first couple to a characteristic inherent in female *and* male human nature. Thus women are exonerated from their legacy as daughters of Eve who are blamed for the advent of sin.

The Corporate Nature of Sin

Schleiermacher's concept of a universal sinfulness that exists prior to every actual sin also illuminates his understanding of the corporate nature of sin. Humans are "guilty of original sin" in that we are born into the corporate life of humanity, a life formed in part through the sins of previous generations. In our corporate existence, sinfulness "operates in every individual through the sin and sinfulness of others." However, in contrast to the traditional belief that original sin is transmitted individually from parent to child during sexual intercourse, transmission occurs through the influence of our actions upon each other within the corporate nature of human existence. Sin is found "in each the work of all, and in all the work of each; and only in this corporate character, indeed, can it [sin] be properly and fully understood." Sin is conveyed by our individual free choices in relationships and "implanted" within others; sin does not exist apart from relationships.[13]

Following this nontraditional conception of the corporate transmission of a universal sinfulness that precedes action, Schleiermacher disagrees with applying the term "original sin" only to the sin of the first human pair. Rather, two terms, "originated original sin" and "originating original sin," should be applied to the relationship between generations.[14] Our parents' actual sins become the "originated original sin" we inherit when we are born into the interconnected corporate life of humanity. This inheritance is "sufficient ground" for our own actual sins that we commit through our own free choice.[15] "Actual sin" is "a manifestation of the universal sinfulness, and [it] represents a victory, though but momentary or partial, of flesh over spirit."[16] Our actual sins then become the "originating original sin" for the next generation, and so the process of sin continues. This doctrine of the origin and transmission of sin is thoroughly embedded in Schleiermacher's concept of the inherent interdependence of all creation. Thus he logically defines original sin as "the corporate act and the corporate guilt of the human race" due to "the personal guilt of every individual who shares in it."[17]

Both Augustine and Schleiermacher posit notions of original sin based on the interconnectedness of all humanity. Augustine understands the basis of this interconnectedness to be the "vitiated seeds" of Adam inherited by sexual intercourse. In contrast, Schleiermacher locates this interconnectedness in the relationship between generations and in the structure of human development: our self-consciousness precedes our God-consciousness. Rather than our inheriting "seeds," the "germ" of sin is present prior to the development of our God-consciousness in "an independent activity of the flesh" that will in time develop as "resistance to the spirit."[18]

Sexuality is not specified as the problem in the "independent activity of the flesh," and Schleiermacher's development of interconnectedness does not depend on sexual intercourse for transmission. Thus by implication, his work breaks the connection between sin and procreation and exonerates sexual desire from its traditional designation as the penalty for original sin. Schleiermacher explicitly exonerates sexual desire in his discussion of the notion of the "virgin birth" of Jesus: "The notion must not be based upon—and just as little made the basis of—a condemnation of the sexual impulse, as if its satisfaction were something sinful and productive of sin."[19]

Thus Schleiermacher's position removes the burden of fault from women. To deny the actions of the first pair as the cause of sin in each succeeding generation is to deny that Eve, the first woman, is responsible for the miseries of human existence.[20] Schleiermacher's position implies that women and men are equally responsible for committing actual sins that are inherited by succeeding generations. To deny that Eve is responsible for human misery undercuts Luther's belief that a wife should be subordinated to her husband as "punishment" for Eve's role in the advent of sin. To deny that husbands have theological justification to punish their wives is one step toward repudiating the belief that husbands may use violence if necessary to enforce this punishment. Just as Schleiermacher refutes the belief that the sin of all succeeding generations is due to the actions of the first pair, we should also discard the belief that all succeeding generations of wives must submit to abuse from their husbands due to the punishment of Eve.[21]

Schleiermacher's doctrine of sin also provides an alternative theological basis for understanding why the cultural practice of wife beating has been pervasive for more than two thousand years of Western history. As noted above, this practice has been justified traditionally by the belief that women are more responsible than men for the fall to sin, and that God decreed that all wives must submit to their husbands due to the punishment of Eve, the first "wife." In contrast, Schleiermacher's conception that the corporate life of humanity is formed in part through the sins of previous generations suggests that the acts of violence committed by each generation of husbands are inherited as the basis for violent actions by husbands in the succeeding generation. Schleiermacher's understanding of corporate humanity illuminates how the physical abuse of wives by husbands is a corporate problem. It cannot be explained as isolated instances of individual wives failing to be submissive.

Sin as Estrangement

In Tillich's theological system, anxiety and estrangement are the conditions of sin that describe human existence. There is nothing in women's nature that makes them more susceptible to or responsible for sin. Tillich's analysis of sin disassociates sin from sexuality[22] and further contributes to the new paradigm of marriage as mutual empowerment because his view of human existence can be used to describe the anxiety of becoming a self in a relationship of mutuality. His work also illuminates why women who choose self-denial have been considered virtuous and why battered wives who choose to leave their abusive husbands have been considered sinful and counseled to return.[23]

Estrangement Holds Women and Men Equally Accountable

In contrast to Schleiermacher's analysis of the corporate nature of sin, Tillich develops his doctrine of sin from a psychological interpretation of the individuals in the Genesis 3 story. The most important part of this story is the prohibition against eating the fruit, because this prohibition is evidence of a division of consciousness between the Creator and the creatures prior to the creatures' act of eating. This division "presupposes a sin which is not yet sin but which is also no longer innocence. It is the desire to sin."[24] The yearning to sin is the precondition of sin in this division of consciousness between God and the humans, not the "weaker nature" of Eve. In contrast to Augustine's and Luther's interpretations of Genesis 3 that make Eve (and subsequently all women) more responsible than Adam for the existence of sin, Tillich's interpretation holds Eve and Adam equally accountable: "In the Genesis story the two sexes and nature, represented by the serpent, work together."[25]

Tillich names the "Fall" as the transition from "essence," defined as unity with God, to "existence," defined as estrangement from God. In contrast to traditional interpretations of Genesis 3, this essence of humanity is a psychological state of "dreaming innocence," rather than a historical moment. The state of dreaming innocence has no time or place in history because it "has potentiality, not actuality." However, a concrete example of this innocence is a psychological state in "the early stages of a child's development." The state of dreaming innocence or unrealized possibilities "drives beyond itself" because it is not "perfection." Only a conscious unity of essence and existence would be perfect, and this is the case only for God, who "transcends essence and existence." In contrast to God, all creatures are finite, and as humans, we are aware of our finitude, our "finite freedom." We experience this awareness as "anxiety" because we realize we are "a mixture of being and non-being," and we are "threatened by non-being."[26]

This state of anxiety or awareness of finitude is experienced as the "temptation" to choose the transition from essence to existence. Either choice is perceived as a loss of self: Tillich writes, "Man experiences the anxiety of losing himself by not actualizing himself and his potentialities and the anxiety of losing himself by actualizing himself and his potentialities. . . . The anxiety of this situation is the state of temptation. Man decides for self-actualization, thus producing the end of dreaming innocence."[27] Anxiety provides the opportunity for the transition from essence to existence, and in our finite freedom we make the decision for actualization, for existence. The state of existence is the condition of sin because now we are estranged from God as well as from "other beings" and from ourselves; prior to our transition to existence, we were united with God in the state of essence. Tillich retains the word "sin" for the decision to exist because "sin" denotes personal responsibility for this decision.[28] Thus as humans we are aware of infinity and of being excluded from infinity. The human creature is caught in the anxiety of losing self by not actualizing his or her own possibilities, and of losing self by actualizing these possibilities. Actualization will mean estrangement from God, which is the human condition of sin for both men and women.

Although Tillich's concept of existence as estrangement is problematic in a relational world in which existence is defined as being constituted by relationships,[29] his view of sin can illuminate the anxiety of becoming a self in a relationship of deep mutuality with an intimate partner. In the beginning of a new intimate relationship, the couple can be in a psychological state of "dreaming innocence" in the sense that they do not know each other very well. The development of intimacy, the process of knowing and being known, is just beginning. The intimate relationship has potential but is not yet actual. As described in chapters 1 and 2 of this book, practicing relational power is a challenge and mutuality is a process filled with tension and fear. Each partner is struggling to give up control, share power, overcome the fear of being loved for who he or she is becoming, and recognize and honor differences.

Anxiety can develop because one fears the loss of self in this process. In refusing the relationship, one loses the possibilities of the self one could become in the relationship. Yet if one enters the relationship, one fears losing the self one has become prior to the relationship or the possibilities the self could realize in other relationships. However, here the application of Tillich's doctrine of sin breaks down, because in a relational world, humans are not estranged from God. Rather, humans can choose to receive the possibilities God offers in each moment of existence.[30]

Self-Actualization, Women's Experience, and Battered Wives

In contrast to Tillich, who does not distinguish between men and women in his understanding of human experience and sin, Judith Plaskow argues that Tillich ultimately describes only male experience. Whereas the *refusal* to become a self is not named as sin in Tillich's theology, women are excluded because Plaskow believes (following the work of Valerie Saiving) that the most common sin of women is the denial of self.[31] Tillich's definition of sin as self-actualization "makes it difficult to understand how or why the failure to be self-actualizing would be considered sinful at all, and thus undercuts his specific remarks on self-estrangement which are relevant to women's experience."[32]

Similar to Plaskow's definition of women's most common sin as self-denial, Mary Daly and Jane Caputi define the "original sin of women" as low self-esteem, self-hatred, and guilt that women develop due to their collusion with the role of subordination. Women's original sin is the "state of complicity in patriarchal oppression that is inherited by women through socialization processes; socially transmitted dis-ease involving psychological paralysis, low Self-esteem, hatred of Self, emotional dependence, horizontal violence, and a never ending conviction of one's own guilt."[33] Daly's and Caputi's analysis of how women inherit the sin of self-hatred by accepting subordination provokes further examination of Tillich's doctrine of sin in relation to women.

It is not only because women in patriarchal societies are socialized to deny themselves that Tillich's definition of sin (as the choice for self-existence) excludes the possibility of naming women's self-denial as sin. Tillich's doctrine also excludes women because in patriarchy, women who choose self-denial are deemed virtuous.[34] Tillich's doctrine excludes women's experience of being celebrated as virtuous for self-denial because according to Tillich, the failure to decide among potentialities produces not virtue, but anxiety that is the precondition of sin: "Man experiences the anxiety of losing himself by not actualizing himself and his potentialities."[35]

In contrast to these examples of how women's experiences of self-denial are not included in Tillich's doctrine of sin, I hold that Tillich's doctrine *does* include women's experience of anxiety and being named sinful when they do choose self-actualization. For example, Tillich's doctrine of sin illuminates how women who become battered wives are deemed sinful for choosing self-actualization by leaving their abusive husbands. Until this century, the vast majority of Western women were kept in a state of "dreaming innocence," a perpetual childhood of "unrealized potentials," by a culture that denied them higher education and, when they became wives, grouped them with children as having no rights before the law. The "essence" of true womanhood was to become a wife at home, happily obedient and dependent on her husband, who would provide for all her needs. This ideal of the protected wife at home was offered to women of all classes yet seldom realized by the majority of women who were not in the upper classes.

This ideal of the wife at home is shattered for the battered wife. Her experience of how her growing anxiety leads to estrangement from her husband parallels Tillich's analysis of how anxiety leads to the choice for estranged existence as a self. As the cycle of violence continues, the wife's anxiety for her very existence increases until finally she leaves. Now she is estranged from her husband, the man whom traditional theology taught her to consider as being more godlike, as more "in God's image," than herself. By leaving, a wife claims her life as worthy of existence; she claims her self. And by leaving her husband and her home, she commits sin according to the rules of patriarchy. Thus family, friends, and clergy who follow these rules admonish her to repent of this sin and return to her husband.

In contrast, theological support for battered wives who leave their husbands can be found in Tillich's concept of the "courage to be"—that is, the courage to choose to become a self even though this choice is named as sin. The courage to be is "the ethical act in which man affirms his own being in spite of those elements of his existence which conflict with his essential self-affirmation."[36] Similar to Tillich's concept of the "courage to be," Daly and Caputi encourage women to have the "Courage to Sin," to repudiate the low self-esteem and self-hatred that define their understanding of women's original sin. This courage is "the Courage to trust and Act on one's own deepest intuitions."[37] One battered wife who left her husband exhibits such courage as she acts on her deepest intuitions for self-survival: "Getting the strength came with my finally deciding that I was dying, and that if I was going to die, I was going to die fighting, which meant I had to leave."[38] This woman claimed her "self," her right to life free from violence.

Overcoming Sin with Sexual Love

In addition to illuminating the experience of battered wives and the anxiety of becoming a self in a relationship of mutuality, Tillich's doctrine of sin also provides a resource for disassociating sin with sexuality.[39] Sexuality is not corrupted with sin; rather, sexuality is a medium for revealing the "mystery of being" that "manifests its relation to us in a special way" through the sexual.[40] The definition of sin as estrangement provides a logical context for Tillich's understanding of sexuality as a medium or point of connection with the sacred because sexual intimacy is a means of union, of overcoming estrangement. Although this understanding of sexuality is mentioned by Tillich only in a footnote, his understanding provides a point of departure for contemporary theologians and ethicists who have associated sexuality with the sacred.[41] Tillich's association of sexuality with the sacred in the context of his conception of the unity of body and soul is developed in the next chapter.

In Tillich's doctrine of sin, sexuality becomes sinful "concupiscence" only when the sexual drive is "unlimited," that is, not directed toward a particular subject and not united with love. Sexuality as concupiscence seeks only its own pleasure through another, whereas sexual love seeks union with another subject out of desire for that subject. Concupiscence is one of Tillich's three categories of sin or "marks of estrangement." In the classical definition, concupiscence referred to unlimited desire not only for sex, but also for food, knowledge, power, material wealth, and spiritual values. Against the backdrop of this "all-embracing" definition, Tillich believes that Christian theologians, including both Augustine and Luther, have made the error of "the tendency to identify concupiscence with sexual desire." Tillich is particularly critical of the reformers who "do not always clearly reject the un-Protestant doctrine that 'hereditary' sin is rooted in sexual pleasure in the act of propagation." This reduction of concupiscence to sexual desire has contributed to an ambiguous attitude toward sex in Christianity, resulting in the construction of sexuality as a "central ethical and religious problem" that the Christian church has never adequately addressed.[42]

Tillich's analysis of the concept of sexuality within the Christian tradition is important for three reasons. First, he not only repudiates the traditional connection between sexuality and sin; he also associates sexuality with the sacred. Second, his reclaiming of the wider definition of concupiscence places sexual desire within the larger context of fundamental human desires, rather than designating sexual desire in particular as bearing the penalty of sin. Third, Tillich's designation of the *unlimited* nature of desire as the mark of sin provides a theological basis for affirming sexual desire as good when it is limited—that is, when it is directed toward a particular subject and united with love. Tillich offers an ideal of love for intimate partners: "Love as the striving for the reunion of the separated is the opposite of estrangement. In faith and love, sin is conquered because estrangement is overcome by reunion."[43]

Sin as Violence against Creation

Reversing the Tradition of Sin as against God

While Tillich defines unlimited desire as a mark of sin, Suchocki examines the role of violence in creating sin. Augustine's development of original sin as "prideful rebellion against God, affecting all humanity with vice" endured for many centuries because his position effectively answered the question, "How is the experience of suffering, ill-doing, and meaninglessness to be reconciled with the conviction that the world is the good creation of a good God?"[44] Similarly, Suchocki's definition of sin as "unnecessary violence" against the well-being of creation is important for the new paradigm of marriage as mutual empowerment because this definition can effectively answer the question, How is the pervasiveness of violence against wives to be reconciled with the conviction that Christian marriage is the good creation of a good God? Suchocki's work exposes the justification for violence against wives implied in the order of creation that places husbands over wives due to sin. Therefore, verses such as Genesis 3:16, "Your [the woman's] desire shall be for your husband, and he shall rule over you," and Ephesians 5:22, "Wives, be subject to your husbands as you are to the Lord," should not be interpreted as prescriptive. Rather, these verses are descriptive of marital relations in societies structured by the ordering of human relations that are the result of human sin. Since this is not the order of creation that God intended, it should not be the model of marital relations today.[45]

In the dominant Christian tradition, sin has been understood as an attitude or action of rebellion against God—for example, pride and self-centeredness. Suchocki reverses the tradition by positing that sin is primarily an act of rebellion against creation and secondarily an act against God.[46] Pride is then the means of justifying our violent behavior, and self-centeredness is the refusal to transcend our inherited state of unnecessary violence as the means of survival.[47] Suchocki defends her definition of sin by naming seven "difficulties" with historical Christian definitions of sin as rebellion against God. Three of these difficulties are particularly helpful in exposing traditional theological justifications for an order of creation that places husbands over wives and, by implication, justifies the use of violence against wives to maintain this order.

First, the "devaluation of creation" is one difficulty with defining sin as rebellion against God. This definition of sin is based on a hierarchal view of existence that places creation at the bottom, God at the top, and humans in between. In this structure, one can only rebel, and therefore sin, against those higher than oneself in the order of creation. Because acts of harm against the well-being of creation are not considered sin, the implication is that creation "is not significant enough that crimes directly intended against its well-being should merit the name of sin."[48]

Suchocki's analysis exposes the theological underpinnings of failing to name violence against wives as sin because the traditional hierarchical view that places humans above creation also places husbands above wives. Therefore, crimes committed by a man against his wife are less likely to "merit the name of sin." However, the behavior of wives can be named rebellious and therefore sinful. In the predominant Western Christian tradition, there is no parallel notion that the husband can rebel against the authority of the wife. In the case of husbands and wives, accepting a hierarchal order of creation functions to protect the husband's power to enforce this order.

Second, defining sin as rebellion against God "tends to interpret rebellion against any form of political, social, or personal power as a rebellion against God."[49] This conception of rebellion explains why wives are considered to be sinful if they are not subordinate to their husbands. As discussed in the previous chapters, husbands in traditional Christian marriage have not only been given power over wives; the husband's authority has been associated with divine authority (Eph. 5:22).

A contemporary image that illustrates the husband's authority as sanctioned by divine authority is the "divine order." Utilizing a series of umbrellas, the largest umbrella is labeled "God." Under the "God" umbrella is a smaller umbrella labeled "Husband," and under "Husband" is a still smaller umbrella labeled "Wife." Under all three umbrellas is a large hand, reinforcing the view that this order is God's will.[50] Suchocki's analysis of all rebellion as sin against God illuminates why some Christians today believe it is sinful to challenge the order portrayed in this image and also why some clergy would counsel battered wives to return to their abusive husbands. God has placed husbands in power and authority over wives, and therefore wives must submit to husbands. The crux of the issue is the association of the husband's authority with divine authority, and acts of violence may be tolerated in order to maintain this authority.

A third difficulty with defining sin as rebellion against God is that "it also renders invisible the very real and often intended victims of sin. This adds to the violation of these victims, and hence increases rather than explains the sins from which they suffer."[51] Suchocki's analysis of the invisibility and increased suffering of the victim is particularly applicable to battered wives. Rather than acknowledging she is the victim of the sin of violence, all too often the battered wife is told that she is guilty of the sin of disobedience. In a society that structures the ideal wife as submissive and obedient, the wife who is beaten bears the marks of having "failed" to achieve this ideal. Typically, she is made to believe that if she had just behaved differently, her body and spirit would not be bruised and broken. In the words of one victim of spousal abuse: "Everyone I have gone to for help has somehow wanted to blame me and vindicate my husband. I can see it lying there between their words and at the end of their sentences. The clergyman, the doctor, the counselor, my friend's husband, the police—all of them have found a way to vindicate my husband."[52]

The battered wife seeks to be invisible literally, hiding her bruises behind dark glasses and clothes that cover all parts of her body, or hiding behind the walls of her own home: "Few people have ever seen my black and blue face or swollen lips because I have always stayed indoors afterwards, feeling ashamed,"admits one woman.[53] The battered wife suffers in silence and shame because to tell of her abuse would be to "confess" her sin of disobedience or rebellion against her husband, against God. Her silence and shame prevent her from seeking help, and thus she suffers again and again the terror and pain of her husband's abuse as she comes to believe she is the one guilty of wrongdoing: "The feeling of helplessness is due to the fact that it was my fault that I got battered, which I think is common that a woman is blamed because she provoked him."[54] In contrast, defining sin as unnecessary violence against creation puts the burden of justification on those who commit violence against any creature; this definition makes visible the victimization of the battered wife and the sin of the abusive husband's violent behavior.

Alternative Views for the Transmission of Original Sin

Similar to her reversal of the tradition regarding the nature of sin, Suchocki also differs from the tradition regarding the transmission of original sin. In contrast to the traditional concept that original sin is inherited through sexual intercourse, she offers three alternative modes of transmission unrelated to sexual expression: "a propensity toward violence," "an interrelational solidarity of the human species," and "social structures that shape the formation of consciousness and conscience."[55] Thus, similar to Schleiermacher and Tillich, Suchocki's position does not associate the transmission of sin with sexuality, procreation, or women.

The first mode of transmission, the human "propensity toward violence," is our inheritance of "aggressive instincts" from ancestors for whom violence was necessary for survival.[56] Using archeological evidence, scientist Christoph Wasserman theorizes that because our vegetarian ancestors could not survive successive droughts, only our meat-eating ancestors survived by violently killing animals and each other.[57] Building on Wasserman's work and the evolutionary explanation of sin developed by Schleiermacher, Suchocki posits that as "hominids" developed through time to become humans, they developed the capability to transcend violence through "empathy, memory, and imagination." Following this development, the acts of violence previously necessary for survival became unnecessary. Yet we humans continue to commit unnecessary violence, and this is sin.[58]

The work of scientist Irenaeus Eibl-Eibesfeldt establishes the universality of violent behavior among members of every human community. Eibl-Eibesfeldt supports his position against critics by citing the "acceptability" of violence toward wives in societies judged "peaceful" on the basis of the behavior of males toward other males.[59] Suchocki observes that the judgment of "peacefulness" based on the behavior of men toward each other implies the "androcentric bias of

[the] critics."[60] I suggest that this judgment also implies the acceptability of wives as the "appropriate victims" of violence. Violent acts against wives were acceptable and appropriate to the degree that these acts were rendered invisible in these cultures designated as "peaceful."

The second mode of transmission is through the solidarity of the human race. This solidarity is based in Whitehead's doctrine of internal relations: every being is constituted by its relationships with every other entity in creation. This interconnectedness of all beings "mediates the effects of violence throughout the race,"[61] and one response to our ongoing conscious and unconscious experiences of violence is anxiety.[62] Thus in disagreement with Tillich's notion that anxiety is a state that precedes sin, Suchocki declares that anxiety is a result of sin as unnecessary violence. However, anxiety can also be a positive motivation for change: "Anxiety can become the catalyst that signals the wrongness of the stereotype into which one is forced. Anxiety can be a first step toward liberation."[63]

Suchocki's analysis of anxiety is particularly pertinent for women who are suffering violence from their husbands. Here the "wrongness of the stereotype" demands that the wife be submissive and obedient to her husband. Yet if a woman who is being beaten denies or remains silent about her anxiety in order to stay in the relationship, she is jeopardizing her very life. One woman who survived writes: "He hit you again. You can't remember where. Your back, your ribs, your spine. All you could say was, 'Stop! Please stop! What are you doing?' He said he was ending his pain, stopping the pain for good. Sometime between the punches and kicks to your back with his hands around your throat, you realized he meant you."[64] In contrast to Tillich, who postulates that the anxiety of losing oneself influences one to sin, battered wives are anxious and fearful that their loss of self, their death, is imminent as a result of sin, the sin of violence perpetrated against them. For battered wives, acting on their anxiety to get help is indeed the "first step toward liberation."

In addition to the physical violence, wives who are beaten also suffer psychic violence. Suchocki defines psychic violence as "the stereotyping that tends to demean the self-image of the other, and restrict self-development possibilities for the other; and therefore, of course, to rob of the other's future."[65] This definition of psychic violence parallels the testimony of women who have been beaten by their husbands: "I want to speak to women who, like me, don't yet have the strength to fight from where they are; . . . who feel humiliated and ashamed at being used as they are, . . . and [who] still allow themselves to be used and abused, and will again, because we half believe as we have been told, that we deserve no better."[66] A woman who believes that she does not "deserve" a life free from marital violence is a woman who believes her future can be no different from her present. By associating the demeaning of another's self-image with psychic violence and naming this violence as sin, Suchocki provides a theological basis for recognizing violence against wives as sin. This recognition reverses the tradition that has most often attributed guilt to the receiver of marital violence rather than to the perpetrator of the violence.

The third mode of transmission is the social institutions that forcefully shape human "consciousness and conscience."[67] As corporate entities, institutions can become powerful vehicles for racism, sexism, and other structures of sin because institutions constitute the persons who participate in them.[68] For example, the social structures of racism and sexism are inherited, and, similar to Schleiermacher's view of the corporate nature of sin, these structures shape the formation of ethical beliefs and actions of each generation. Because these institutional structures protect the privileges of the group in power, they are difficult to dismantle and they persist through time.[69]

Suchocki's analysis of the role of institutions in the transmission of sin illuminates one reason why the practice of wife beating has persisted throughout the centuries. The institution of traditional marriage functions to protect the privileges of men by giving husbands authority over wives. This authority has included the "right of chastisement" and the invisibility of wives before the law. The political, economic, and religious authority of husbands "over" wives has been institutionalized in the patriarchal family, and this male authority provides the basis for acts of violence against wives.[70] One battered wife names the social structural component in her experience: "As a married woman I have no recourse but to remain in the situation which is causing me to be painfully abused. I have suffered physical and emotional battering and spiritual rape because the social structure of my world says I cannot do anything about a man who wants to beat me."[71]

Another aspect of the transmission of sin through institutions is how the children are shaped by the "hypocrisies" that a society perpetuates "to hide the violence of the privileged." The children inherit and are formed by the hypocrisies even before the children are consciously able to choose their beliefs and behaviors. This inheritance "is analogous to the traditional doctrine of original sin, where all persons since Adam are corrupted by sin before they have the means to exercise either consent or denial toward the corrupting sin."[72] The concept of the "sanctity of marriage" is one example of these hypocrisies that "hide the violence of the privileged." Until as recently as 1981, when the law changed, belief in the sanctity of marriage deterred lawmakers and law enforcement officials from intervening to arrest husbands who committed acts of violence against their wives. Similarly, some clergypersons have counseled battered wives and their children to remain in life-threatening situations in order to preserve the sanctity of marriage. The ramifications for children of preserving this sanctity are sometimes brutal. For example, 63 percent of young men ages eleven to twenty who are incarcerated for homicide are there because they killed their mother's batterer.[73]

Repudiating Violence against Wives

By proposing doctrines of sin that break the traditional association of sin with the body, sexuality, and women, the three theologians discussed in this chapter offer theological resources for repudiating violence against wives in Christian marriage.

Schleiermacher defines sin as anything that "arrests" the development of God-consciousness. And although he names the propensity to sin as the strength of habit in the "flesh," the problem is self-centeredness, not sexuality. Schleiermacher redefines original sin as the corporate action and corporate guilt of the human race with no implication of sexual desire as tainted with sin. By locating the transmission of sin through the inheritance of each preceding generation's actual sins, Schleiermacher repudiates the association of procreation with sin. Denying the actions of Adam and Eve as the cause of sin, Schleiermacher holds women and men equally responsible for committing the actual sins inherited by the next generation. Thus Schleiermacher's doctrine of sin does not implicate women as guiltier than men for the existence of sin.

Schleiermacher denies that the actions of Adam and Eve are the cause of sin in each generation. This denial undercuts the belief that each generation of wives should be subordinated to their husbands as punishment for Eve's role in the beginning of sin. Denying this punishment also denies that husbands may use violence if necessary to enforce the punishment. Schleiermacher's conception that the corporate life of humanity is formed in part by the inheritance of the sins of previous generations provides an alternative theological basis for understanding why the practice of violence against wives has been so pervasive throughout human history. Each generation of husbands inherits the acts of violence committed by the previous generation of husbands. Thus violence against wives must be addressed as a corporate problem rather than as a problem of individual wives failing to be submissive.

In contrast to Schleiermacher's conception of sin that focuses on the interconnectedness of humanity, Tillich defines sin as estrangement from God, self, and others. This estrangement is the result of the transition from the state of "essence" that is unity with God to the state of "existence" that is separation from God. Tillich offers a psychological interpretation of the actions of Adam and Eve in which each of them is held equally accountable for the advent of sin. Sexuality is not implicated as sinful; rather, sexuality is one of the media of divine revelation. Tillich's conception of sexuality as a point of connection with the sacred is a logical extension of his definition of sin as estrangement because sexual intimacy is a means of union, of overcoming estrangement.

Tillich's doctrine of sin can be used to explain why battered wives are judged as committing sin if they leave their husbands. According to Tillich, sin is the result of the transition from the state of "dreaming innocence" to the state of estranged existence as a self, a transition initiated by anxiety. Similarly, as a battered wife's growing anxiety for her very survival increases, she makes the decision to leave, to become estranged from her husband. Her decision to choose the survival of herself is named sin by those who accept the patriarchal belief that women should deny themselves. In contrast, Tillich's theology offers support to battered wives who choose to leave. His concept of the "courage to be" affirms the choice of self regardless of one's life situation.

Suchocki redefines sin as "unnecessary violence" and as an act of rebellion against creation rather than against God. She posits the transmission of sin through three modes: our inheritance of a human bent toward violence, the inter-relationality of the human race, and social structures that shape human awareness and moral convictions. Applying Whitehead's theory that we are constituted by our relationships, Suchocki argues that groups and societies can become powerful vehicles for transmitting racism, sexism, and other structures of sin that influence us even before we have the consciousness to choose. These three modes of the transmission of sin are unrelated to sexuality, and women are not held to be more responsible than men for the advent and continuation of sin.

Suchocki's critique of the traditional definition of sin as violence against God is helpful in analyzing the theological basis used to legitimize violence against wives. Through the association of husbands with God, the traditional notion of sin as rebellion against God has been used to condone violence against wives who "sin" by rebelling against their husbands. Suchocki's work also illuminates why violence against wives has been pervasive even in Christian families. She posits that the transmission of sin occurs through our inheritance of a human bent toward violence and the solidarity—or interconnectedness—of both the human species and our social institutions. The cultural practice of wife beating has been inherited by each succeeding generation through the institution of traditional marriage.

Sin, Power, and a Relational World

This chapter has examined understandings of sin that do not implicate the body, sexuality, or women. These understandings provide a doctrine of sin that can promote mutuality in marriage by holding men and women equally accountable for sin, associating sexuality with the sacred, and illuminating how violence against wives is sin. Analysis of the power relations in the traditional hierarchal order of creation that places husbands above wives exposes the justification for violence against wives implied in this hierarchy. This hierarchy is the result of sin and thus should not be promoted as the ideal model for Christian couples today. Rather, by practicing relational power and mutuality, couples have the opportunity to model their relationship on the order of creation that God intended.

In contrast to doctrines that understand sin in terms of the hierarchical order of creation, the doctrine I propose is grounded in a view of the interrelatedness of all creation, including God. God is present in every moment, offering the best possibility for that moment to promote redemption or creative transformation toward the good. Building on the doctrines of sin proposed by Schleiermacher and Suchocki, I define sin as denying or tearing the connections in the interrelatedness of creation by causing harm to oneself, other humans, or nonhuman creatures. When we cause harm, we are rejecting the best possibility that God is offering us in that moment because the possibility that God offers is always toward creating the good, the well-being of all creatures.

When we choose to misuse our creative power to harm ourselves and other creatures, we also harm God because part of God's nature is determined in response to the actions of the world. We are therefore in a reciprocal relationship of cocreation with God, not a hierarchical one. In the hierarchical model, an all-powerful God is at the top and each one's duty is to obey the more powerful authorities above who exercise control of those below. In a relational world, the hierarchy is turned on its side so that power flows from God to creatures *and* from creatures to God. Just as God influences the world, so the world influences God. However, God's influence on the world is limited by sin because sin includes the refusal to join one's power with God to create the best possible good in the given moment.

Two kinds of sin can be distinguished: personal and contextual. Personal sin is the misuse of one's personal power to cause harm. This misuse occurs because each generation inherits a proclivity for self-centeredness from the preceding generation. This self-centeredness is based in the desire for self-preservation and survival. Although violence against others was necessary for the survival of our earliest ancestors, human imagination and creativity have evolved so that we can now conceive other strategies for survival and conflict resolution. John B. Cobb Jr. has referred to sin as a lack of imagination. Thus we sin when we continue to use violence and other means to harm each other.

Through the misuse of personal power, humans have created and continue to perpetuate corporate structures of evil that create contexts for predisposing humans to sin. These institutions are based in a hierarchical model of society and, as Suchocki has argued, function as a means of protecting the privileges and power of the dominant group. Therefore, original sin is more adequately termed contextual sin because the sin we inherit is reproduced by these social structures that perpetuate contexts of evil, influencing both our conscious and unconscious choices.[74] For example, one can sin unconsciously when one chooses to act in a racist manner without being aware that one is racist. This can occur when one has not had any life experience that confronts one's attitude or behavior as racist.

The current structures of racism, sexism, classism, militarism, and other forms of oppression enable some persons to use their power to harm creation. These same structures function to convince other persons that they have no power, and thus these persons perpetuate sin by failing to use their power. For example, the imbalance of social and economic power between husbands and wives in the traditional structure of marriage can lead to the husband committing acts of violence against the wife and the wife feeling unable to use her power to leave.

Some persons are born (or marry) into contexts of abuse and oppression in which the amount of evil negates many opportunities for the realization of human potential. The choices made by previous generations are felt as great obstacles in these contexts. We do have a choice as to how we will use our creative power, yet this choice is strongly informed by our context, just as God's offering of possibilities is limited by the actions of entities in this world. However, God does not abandon us. Rather, God receives the obstacles into God's being and responds by continuing to offer us optimal possibilities to overcome the obstacles.[75] Overcoming the obstacles of structural oppression will take the cooperation of many individuals and groups because many cooperate to perpetuate these structures.

My definition of contextual sin locates our human predisposition to sin in the social structures we inherit, not in our bodies. Thus the body and sexuality should not be associated with sin since human beings inherit the sin of our ancestors through corporate structures of evil, not through corrupted human nature. These structures, such as racism and sexism, impact our intimate relationships and create contexts that predispose us to sin against those closest to us in the interrelatedness of creation.

My definition of contextual sin also challenges the traditional designation of uncontrolled sexual desire as the penalty for original sin. To name uncontrolled desire as sin is to make control a virtue. Yet following Suchocki's analysis of the hierarchy of creation, making control a virtue in a society structured by this hierarchy empowers those who seek to control others "below" them. Thus, rather than associating sin with uncontrolled sexual desire, I hold that sin is operative in the desire to control others, particularly when violence is used to enforce this control.

Finally, in contrast to Augustine, who asserted that humans sin due to the inheritance of bodies corrupted by the vitiated seeds transmitted through sexual intercourse, I contend that the whole person is corrupted by social intercourse with conditions such as abuse, fear, and violence. We choose evil due to experiences that damage us, not because we are born with corrupted natures that cannot choose good.[76] Augustine locates sin in the rational will. I agree that the will is involved because sin is the result of a conscious or unconscious choice to misuse one's will, that is, one's power of creation. I disagree, however, that the will can be considered distinct from other aspects of the human person. Rather, thoughts, feelings, and will are formed through bodily perceptions of the world, and all are integrated to comprise the human personality. The will is not a separate agent. For example, I can will my body to perform a certain act, and yet the content of my will is partially determined by my bodily perceptions of the world as loving or abusive.

Today many Christians recognize that it is time to reject traditional understandings of the role of the body and sexuality in the mediation of sin, and to develop the position that the body and sexuality have positive roles in spiritual development. The next chapter proposes such a development.

CHAPTER FIVE

Body, Sex, and Soul
An Embodied Spirituality of Mutuality

> Rosaura and Pedro are preparing to consummate their marriage for the first time. Except for her face, Rosaura is completely covered with a beautiful white silk sheet. Intricate lace frames a single hole in the sheet, and the sheet has been placed so that this hole is over Rosaura's pubic area. Pedro kneels beside the bed and prays: "Lord, this is not lust or lewdness but to make a child to serve you." As Pedro concludes his prayer, Rosaura reaches for the lamp cord and turns off the light.
>
> *Like Water for Chocolate*[1]

This film scene offers a vivid portrayal of a traditional Christian association of sexuality and women with sin, and the belief that sexuality is separate from and detrimental to spirituality. The association of males with superior soul/spirituality and females with inferior body/ sexuality was established in classical Greek philosophy and incorporated into Christian theology. As discussed in the previous chapter, this conception of male and female humanity has functioned to devalue women, the body, and sexuality and to justify the husband's rule over his wife.[2]

Given the current domestic violence and divorce statistics, we desperately need to reenvision what it means to be human, especially as humans pledged to each other in marriage. Disassociating the body and sexuality from sin is not enough for developing a new paradigm of marriage as mutual empowerment. It is also necessary to address the nature of the relationship between body, soul, sexuality, and spirituality. This chapter develops the position that for Christian couples, understanding the body and sexuality as having positive roles in spiritual development enhances mutuality and repudiates violence against wives. These positive roles for the body and sexuality in spiritual development provide a meeting ground for advancing mutuality and rejecting violence. Emerging from this meeting ground, this chapter proposes an embodied spirituality of mutuality for Christian couples based on the view that the relationship between body and soul, and sexuality and spirituality, is one of mutual reciprocity.

The relationship of mutual reciprocity between body and soul is created through interdependence as body and soul develop together through the exchange of experiences of a human-coming-into-being. Body and soul alternately guide each other: the body depends on the soul as a center of organization, and the soul depends on the body to mediate wisdom and knowledge to the soul. I understand the soul as the aspect of human beings that integrates rational and nonrational feelings, thoughts, desires, intuitions, bodily sensations, memory, ideas, and imagination.[3] As the experiences of soul and body are woven together through time, both sexuality and spirituality are aspects of moments of experience.

Thus I agree with other Christian thinkers who have asserted that sexuality should be associated with spirituality.[4] I define spirituality as our awareness of our interrelatedness—our inherent connection to human and nonhuman creation and to God—and this awareness can be experienced through both body and soul. Both male and female bodies should be held in reverence, for the body has a primary role in spiritual as well as physical development, and sexual intimacy can be a means of experiencing God's love for creation. Therefore, females should not be associated with the body and sexuality, nor should males be associated with the soul and spirituality. Rather, both females and males are fully body and soul—and both are sexual and spiritual beings in each moment of experience. Thus in marriage, the body of each partner should be honored as the couple develops sexual and spiritual intimacy.

This embodied spirituality of mutuality for Christian couples draws on the work of selected thinkers from the Christian tradition, ranging from the medieval to the contemporary period. This range demonstrates that the concept of a positive relationship of mutual reciprocity between body and soul, and sexuality and spirituality, is not a recent innovation in Christian theology. Medieval mystic Julian of Norwich posits that God is "joined" to body and soul, and there is a mutuality of yearning, desire, and will between God and humans. Writing four centuries later, Friedrich Schleiermacher conceives body and soul in a reciprocal relationship as "sensible self-consciousness" and "God-consciousness." In the twentieth century, Paul Tillich argues that sexuality is a "medium of divine revelation," and Rebecca Parker asserts that sexual intimacy can be a "means of grace." Also in the twentieth century, Alfred North Whitehead grounds the positive valuing of the body—understanding that God values it also—in a philosophy that describes the interdependence of body and soul. His work provides an alternative to the classical Greek philosophical view that posited the body as inferior to the soul.

Sacred Body and Sensual Soul

From the beginning of Christianity, the doctrine of the incarnation (the belief that God became human in Jesus) has usually blocked complete negativity toward the body.[5] Julian's positive body theology is grounded in the incarnation, and she uses this doctrine to explain why the body is sacred and the soul is sensual. Julian not only posits reciprocity between body and soul; she also describes how God cares for the body and dwells in the soul. Julian's use of marriage imagery to describe a mutuality of desire and will between God and the soul can provide an ideal for love between married human couples.

The woman known as Julian of Norwich (1342–c. 1423) lived in a sealed cell attached to St. Julian's Church in Norwich, England. Julian formulated her theology of body and soul during the years when the Black Plague swept across Western Europe and England. According to one estimate, half the total population of Norwich died due to the Plague.[6] Julian's defense of human nature as good and her positive body theology perhaps brought some comfort to those who were experiencing so much bodily suffering.

As an anchoress, Julian was considered "dead to the world."[7] Yet her theology is very much alive to this world as she emphasizes God's love for everything God created, including the body.[8] Similar to her own enclosed living space, Julian imagines body and soul together as "enclosed in the goodness of God."[9] The soul is located in the human heart as revealed when "our good Lord opened my spiritual eye, and showed me my soul in the midst of my heart."[10] With the soul in the heart, the enclosure of body and soul is described this way: "The body is clad in the cloth, and the flesh in the skin, and the bones in the flesh, and the heart in the trunk."[11]

As an example of God's esteem for the human body, God's care is graphically described for one of the most basic bodily functions, the movement of the bowels for elimination. Food in human bodies "is shut in as if in a well-made purse," and then "the purse is opened and then shut again, in most seemly fashion." This procedure is evidence that God "does not despise what he has made, nor does he disdain to serve us in the simplest natural functions of our body, for love of the soul which he created in his own likeness."[12] Even though Julian states that only the soul is created in God's likeness, she does not denigrate the body.

The goodness of the human nature, including the body, is revealed in the dual nature of Jesus as both divine and human. As Julian explains, "In Christ our two natures are united, for the Trinity is comprehended in Christ, in whom our higher part is founded and rooted; and our lower part the second person has taken, which nature was first prepared for him."[13] Although Julian uses the imagery of higher and lower to describe human nature, she does not disparage the lower.

Following the unity of divinity and humanity in Christ, God is also "joined" to the lower nature, the flesh of human creatures. Julian's understanding that God is joined to both body and soul is in contrast to Augustine, who asserts that the image of God is only in the higher part of the soul. Furthermore, Julian challenges the traditional conception of conflict between the soul and the body with her proposition that there is nothing but love between the higher and lower natures: "For the life and the power that we have in the lower part is from the higher, and it comes down to us from the substantial love of the self, by grace. In between the one and the other is nothing at all, for it is all one love."[14]

The process of God's joining to both body and soul is the process of the soul becoming sensual and the city of God being established within the soul. Similar to Schleiermacher's conception of human development (as described in the previous chapter), for Julian the beginning of human life and the presence of God in the human soul are simultaneous. The sensual soul is joined to the body, and both soul and body are enclosed in the goodness of God. She writes, "And when our soul is breathed into our body, at which time we are made sensual, at once mercy and grace begin to work. . . . For I saw very surely that our substance is in God, and I also saw that God is in our sensuality." In Julian's imagery, God's presence in the soul constitutes the city of God. In contrast to Augustine, who posits the "City of God" outside of this world, Julian locates this city within the human soul living in this world. She asserts that the human soul was created to be the dwelling place for God and that God will never abandon it: "For in the same instant and place in which our soul is made sensual, in that same instant and place exists the city of God. . . . God is never out of the soul, in which he will dwell blessedly without end."[15]

This city of the soul is "as wide as if it were an endless citadel, and also as if it were a blessed kingdom." This city is ruled by Jesus, who, as fully human and fully divine, is portrayed as the ideal bishop and king: "In the midst of that city sits our Lord Jesus, true God and true man, a handsome person and tall, highest bishop, most awesome king, most honourable Lord. . . . The humanity and the divinity sit at rest, the divinity rules and guards, without instrument or effort."[16] Yet in contrast to the traditional view of the soul ruling over the body, in Julian's imagery soul and body grow together with the aid of gifts from God that are "enclosed" in Jesus "until the time that we are fully grown, our soul together with our body and our body together with our soul." Here again, Julian is perhaps using her own experience of being enclosed as an anchoress to describe how God works through Jesus to enable the development of body and soul. During this growth process, there is a reciprocal relationship between body and soul as they assist each other: "Let either of them [body or soul] take help from the other, until we have grown to full stature as creative nature brings about."[17] The "full stature" of human growth is eternal life. Following the Christian tradition, eternal life is possible because of the incarnation and resurrection of Jesus Christ. "And because of the glorious union which was thus made by God between the soul and the body," writes Julian, "mankind had necessarily to be restored from a double death, which restoration could never be until the time when the second person in the Trinity had taken the lower part of human nature, whose highest part was united to him in its first creation."[18] Julian's positive body theology is grounded in God's love as revealed through the incarnation and resurrection of Jesus Christ. The body is not described as inferior to the soul; rather, body and soul "help" each other grow toward Christian maturity in eternal life.

The fact that God's love and grace are offered equally to women and men provides the theological basis for Julian to perceive women and men as equal before God—equal in both soul and body. Julian does not make a distinction between male bodies and female bodies; both male and female bodies are united with God. She does not associate women with the body, nor does she suggest that women are created for procreation. After analyzing Julian's theology, Eleanor McLaughlin writes: "Beside the now well-documented classical Christian stereotype of the female: misbegotten male, daughter of Eve, temptress, insatiable harlot, nagging, unfaithful, garrulous wife, we have found it possible to see another *persona*—the seeker after God, model of human holiness and divine action, wholly equal with her brother in the pursuit of Christian perfection."[19] Within the context of medieval asceticism, Julian's theology offers this persona for women without denigrating the body or sexuality. Women's bodies are sacred because, like men's bodies, they are co-substantiated with Jesus Christ. Furthermore, sexual imagery is used positively to symbolize union with God through the marriage of the soul with God.

In contrast to Augustine, who associates the body with female and the soul with male, Julian does not assign gender to the body. And, as Luther will do some one hundred years later, she describes the soul as female in her marital imagery. The soul was traditionally understood to be male, relative to the body, because the soul is to rule over the body. Yet the soul was conceived as female relative to God because God rules over the soul. Thus Julian's conception of female soul reinforces the system of males ruling over females, rather than challenging this rule. However, in Julian's theology, the "husband" is free of anger and violence as he and his "wife" relate to one another with mutual love.

Julian uses marriage as an analogy to convey God's love for humanity: "God rejoices that he is our true spouse, and that our soul is his beloved wife."[20] There is no violence in this marital relationship; the husband is never "displeased" with the wife, "for he says: I love you and you love me, and our love will never divide in two."[21] In Julian's imagery, wife and husband are joined together in mutual love. Her view of the soul as "beloved wife" is in contrast to Luther's description of the soul as a "wicked harlot" redeemed "from all her evil" by her marriage to Christ. Thus, although both Julian and Luther use the analogy of marriage to describe the union of the human soul with the Divine, Julian conveys God's great love for the soul as wife without denigrating either the bodies or souls of women, especially women who become wives.

Further evidence for a degree of mutuality rather than complete submission by the "wife" in this "marriage" can be found in the mutual desire and will in the relationship between God and the human soul. God is pleased when the soul desires God and comes to God "naked, openly and familiarly. For this is the loving yearning of the soul through the touch of the Holy Spirit." And God as lover desires the human soul "to adhere to him with all its power, and us always to adhere to his goodness." Furthermore, Julian believed, there is an affinity between God's will and the soul's will to have each other: "We may with reverence ask from our lover all that we will, for our natural will is to have God, and God's good will is to have us, and we can never stop willing or loving until we possess him in the fulness of joy."[22]

With these images of mutual desire and will between God and the human soul as the "beloved" wife of God, Julian offers an ideal of the marital relationship that is in contrast to the traditional ideal of the wife's obedience to the husband's rule. Although these texts could be interpreted as reinforcing the association of the husband with God, the ideal for the husband's behavior is one of love without anger or violence. Therefore, Julian's imagery of the soul's marriage with God can provide an ideal for creating human marital relationships based in mutual love.

Reciprocity between Body and Spirituality

Similar to Julian's theme of mutuality, the possibility for a mutual partnership between the body and spirituality can be found in Schleiermacher's description of the "reciprocal" relationship between "sensible self-consciousness" and "God-consciousness." Schleiermacher's theology is a resource for an embodied spirituality of mutuality for couples because his work values the body and does not posit women or men as inferior. Since he does not associate sensible self-consciousness or God-consciousness with male or female, he does not perpetuate the traditional construction of male soul over female body. Furthermore, the body mediates the world to the soul and thus is essential for the development of spirituality.

Human spirituality is God-consciousness, or the feeling of absolute dependence on God. The goal of God-consciousness is to determine each moment of experience, and this determination could be understood as analogous to the traditional notion that spirit should control flesh. However, God-consciousness requires self-consciousness in order to be temporal. To "make an appearance in time," writes Schleiermacher, God-consciousness requires sensible self-consciousness, and this self-consciousness includes physicality. Whereas God-consciousness has an "ever-unchanging identity," God-consciousness without self-consciousness would result in the loss of the consciousness of self. This loss would "irrevocably destroy the coherence of our existence for our own minds." God-consciousness must always be "conjoined" with sensible self-consciousness, a union that Schleiermacher describes as "a co-existence of the two in the same moment, which of course, unless the Ego is to be split up, involves a reciprocal relation of the two." Thus a relationship of reciprocity exists between sensible self-consciousness, which includes physicality, and God-consciousness or spirituality.[23]

God-consciousness is "excited" by the "consciousness of the world."[24] The "seat" of God-consciousness is the relationship of the spirit to the world because interaction with the world is the only way that the human spirit can develop God-consciousness.[25] Because the body is the point of connection with the world, the body mediates the "stimulating influences of the world upon the spirit."[26] Schleiermacher's conception of the body as necessary for spiritual development is in sharp contrast to Luther, who believed that the body can neither help nor harm the soul.

In contrast to the predominant Christian tradition, Schleiermacher argues that the body is necessary for spiritual development. His construction of the body as mediating the "stimulating influences of the world upon the spirit" provides a basis for valuing the body. Mutuality between spirituality and the body is present in Schleiermacher's description of the "reciprocal" relationship between God-consciousness and self-consciousness. He does not associate God-consciousness or self-consciousness with male or female, nor does he posit a masculine soul set over a feminine body. Thus Schleiermacher's work provides a resource for an embodied spirituality that does not posit women as spiritually, morally, or physically inferior to men.

Building on Schleiermacher's and Alfred North Whitehead's work, I define spirituality as the awareness of being in connection or relationship with God and with all creatures. The body primarily mediates this awareness as the human-coming-into-being has experiences in space and time. This awareness can be nurtured, obstructed, or ignored by one's personal choices and by the social context that influences one's choices. For intimate partners, the partnership or marriage is a primary social context. Thus how each partner treats the other's body has a strong influence on the development of both partners' spirituality because, in a relational world, each partner is being constituted by the partner relationship. Partners who adopt the concept of bodily mediation in the development of spirituality that creates reciprocity between body and soul can be enabled to practice relational power; they have adopted an alternative to the traditional conception of the masculine superior soul ruling over the feminine inferior body. In contrast to the belief that the husband should chastise the wife through physical violence for the good of her soul, both husband and wife should treat each other's body with care and respect in order to promote the spiritual development of each partner and of the couple.

Sexuality as Divine Revelation

Tillich's work is a resource for an embodied spirituality because his concept of sexuality as a means of divine revelation provides a theological basis for asserting that sexuality and spirituality are integrally connected. Thus as couples grow closer through sharing their bodies with each other, they can also be growing closer to God. Tillich's position also contributes to an embodied spirituality because his view of the "Fall" to sin does not disrupt the unity of body and soul, and he does not associate body with female and soul with male.

The unity of body and soul is based in Tillich's psychological understanding of the Fall. In this analysis, temptation is the possibility to choose the transition from essence to existence. This choice is between the being and nonbeing of the whole person, not a conflict between body and soul. Body and soul are not separate; therefore, "mythologically speaking, the fruit of the tree of temptation is both sensuous and spiritual."[27] With this analysis of the Fall, Tillich's monistic doctrine of human nature overcomes the traditional dualistic view.

The body is not "lower" or an entity needing to be controlled by the soul. Rather, body, mind, and soul participate together in "life as spirit" that transcends these three aspects of human beings. Spirit is not just one aspect of life with a particular role. Rather, "[spirit] is the all-embracing function in which all elements of the structure of being participate."[28] Therefore, for Tillich, spirit is manifest in the body as well as the soul. Similar to Julian and Schleiermacher, Tillich does not make a distinction between the bodies and souls of males and females. The spirit moves equally through the bodies and souls of men and women.

Tillich's understanding of body and soul does not denigrate women, nor does his view of sexuality. Sexuality, as well as body and soul, is based in the concept of God as "being-itself" or "the ground of being."[29] Because every being participates in being-itself or God, "almost every type of reality has become a medium of revelation somewhere."[30] Human bodies and souls are included on Tillich's list of mediums of revelation found in nature, and he names sex as one of the "natural events" that can have a "revelatory character."[31] In particular, the use of sexual symbols in Christianity is justified not because sexuality is inherently revealing, but because "the mystery of being . . . through the medium of the sexual manifests its relation to us in a special way."[32] Following this conception of sexuality as a medium of revelation, Protestantism is critiqued for "rejecting sexual symbolism." By rejecting sexual symbols, Protestant denominations are "in danger not only of losing much symbolic wealth but also of cutting off the sexual realm from the ground of being and meaning in which it is rooted and from which it gets its consecration."[33]

As a medium of revelation, sexuality points to the mystery of being in which it is grounded and by which it receives sacred meaning. Thus in an embodied spirituality of mutuality for couples, sexual intimacy becomes one means of developing the spiritual life of the partners because sexuality and spirituality are integrally connected.[34]

Sexual Intimacy as Grace

Rebecca Parker develops the concept of sexuality as a means of divine revelation with her argument that sexual intimacy can be "a primary means of grace."[35] Yet whereas Tillich views sexuality as a means of overcoming the estrangement inherent in existence, Parker claims that positive sexual intimacy is a means of experiencing our profound connectedness with all of creation. Making love can enable us to "feel boundaries falling away between the self and the world."[36] Thus, in a relational world, sexual intimacy offers the possibility for couples to experience interconnectedness not only with each other, but also with the world that includes God. For Christian couples, sexual desire for each other provides a means of experiencing the power and intensity of God's love for creation, a creation that God declared is "good" (Gen. 1:31). Of course, sexual desire can be misused to bring harm to oneself or to another; yet contrary to Augustine's view, sexual desire is not the penalty for original sin. Rather, in an embodied spirituality of mutuality, sexual desire is one way that partners can experience the goodness of the interrelatedness of the world that God created.

Positive sexual intimacy not only enables us to experience a demise of boundaries between self and other; positive sexual intimacy also makes us more aware of our own "personal presence and power," writes Parker, because "we feel our power to give joy to another. We know our presence is a blessing to the world."[37] This is the dual gift of positive sexual intimacy. It not only empowers us to receive a sense of the goodness of our interrelatedness; it also reveals our power to impact the quality of this goodness, particularly in the life of our partner.

As we experience our power to receive and to give joy and pleasure with our partner through sexual intimacy, this intimacy becomes an ideal expression of relational power. As Parker explains, "Sexual intimacy, at its best, teaches us this truth about ourselves: that joy is grounded in relational power."[38] In the new paradigm of marriage as mutual empowerment, experiencing the joy of relational power in sexual intimacy can motivate couples to practice relational power in other areas of their relationship, thus creating more opportunities for redemption through intimacy for the couple and their community. The connection between sexual energy, work, and social activism is clear: "Giving life to ourselves, to another, to a work of imagination or research or a political cause—all forms of giving life to life—are bonded to sexual energy."[39] Thus sexuality can be a means of grace for social as well as individual transformation.[40]

Body and Soul Are Interdependent

In contrast to the theology of Parker, Tillich, and Julian of Norwich, Alfred North Whitehead provides a philosophical basis for the interdependence of body and soul. Because he postulates the body as source of wisdom for the soul, Whitehead's concept of the interdependence of body and soul is important for developing an embodied spirituality of mutuality. The bodies of both husbands and wives should be reverenced because the body has a primary role not only in physical but also in spiritual development. Furthermore, Whitehead does not associate the soul with male or the body with female. Just as the body is not inferior, and woman is not associated with the body, so the wife cannot be considered to be inferior to her husband. The use of violence to enforce her subordination to him on the basis of her inferiority is repudiated.

Foundational to Whitehead's conception of how body and soul are related is his principle that reality is composed of moments of experience, rather than matter.[41] From without, groups of individuals or atoms appear to be things we call matter. From within, things are composed of experiences, most of which are subconscious.[42] As each occasion of experience is coming into being, it has a "physical" aspect through which it receives the influence of the past or actuality, and a "mental" aspect through which it entertains the possibility of novelty. Both body and soul are composed of experiences that have physical and mental aspects, so a simple association of physical with body and mental with soul is not accurate in Whitehead's philosophy.[43]

In addition to the assertion that a process or succession of moments of experience constitutes reality, Whitehead's understanding of creativity is also important for understanding how he conceives the interdependence of body and soul. Since Einstein advanced his formula that energy and mass are convertible, the idea that the world is composed of things that embody energy has been widely accepted. Whitehead enlarged this notion of energy to "creativity" and extended it to all things, including souls and bodies.[44] With this conception of reality as experience and energy or creativity, it follows that there is no metaphysical distinction between bodies and souls. Both have energy and are composed of experiences and thereby have the power to initiate activity.[45]

The body does not simply contain the soul as if the soul were a completed entity placed into a receptacle.[46] Rather, since both body and soul are composed of occasions of experience, they develop together through the interaction of experiences as the human-coming-into-being is created. Just as the embryo does not begin with a miniature complete body, the embryo does not "receive" a complete soul.[47]

Although the mental aspect of every occasion, cellular or psychic, is the occasion's entertainment of new possibilities, the body is organized so as to allow one type of occasion— that which constitutes the soul—to be especially affected by novelty and then to transmit that novelty to successive occasions so that the novelty is cumulative. This accumulation constitutes the soul as a "living person," says Whitehead. As a result, the soul is the locus of the entertainment of ideas for the whole body.[48] Because the body is organized so that bodily sensations or feelings are "poured" into the ongoing moments of the soul, the occasions of experience that constitute the soul can include more elements of bodily experiences than any other individual part of the body.[49] Thus the body depends on the soul as a center of organization for the perceptions of the human being.

Yet simultaneously, the soul depends on the body. The body provides the most immediate and most influential environment for the soul as the body mediates the contemporary world to the soul through experiences of space and time. Whitehead calls this bodily mediation the "withness of the body": "For we feel *with the body*. There may be some further specialization into a particular organ of sensation; but in any case the *'withness' of the body* [Whitehead's emphasis] is an ever present, though elusive, element in our perceptions."[50] Although the soul is not limited to the influence of the bodily environment—for example, the soul can directly comprehend the past through memory—the body is primary because the soul is constituted by the actual world of experience mediated through the body. The soul also depends on the body to provide for the ongoing existence of the soul: "[The] continuity of the soul—so far as concerns consciousness—has to leap gaps in time. We sleep or we are stunned. Yet it is the same person who recovers consciousness. . . . Thus . . . the body in particular provide[s] the stuff for the personal endurance of the soul."[51] Thus the soul depends on the body and the body depends on the soul in a relationship of mutuality.

Body and soul develop through this process of mutuality as body and soul guide each other through shared experiences. Through the body's perceptions of its surroundings, the body guides the soul; the soul receives both the influence of the past and God's best possibility for the person at that moment in the given situation. Yet the soul is free within the context of the present to appropriate the past without being bound to the past. In this way the soul guides the body.

Whitehead's theories extend beyond the individual human being to describe the reciprocal relationship between the soul and the world: "[The] experienced world is one complex factor in the composition of many factors constituting the essences of the soul. . . . [In] one sense the world is in the soul. But antithetical[ly] . . . our experience of the world involves the exhibition of the soul itself as one of the components within the world."[52] Thus Whitehead's metaphysics provides an explanation of the interrelatedness of all creation. The world is a factor in the constitution of the soul, and the soul is one more factor that constitutes the world.

Whitehead's metaphysics of body-soul interdependence overturns the traditional hierarchy of superior soul over inferior body, providing a resource for developing an embodied spirituality of mutuality for couples. The body is not inferior to the soul because both body and soul are constituted by shared experiences in a relationship of reciprocity as body and soul alternately guide each other. And because gender is not assigned to either body or soul, the primacy of the body in daily experience is acknowledged for both husbands and wives as human beings. Freed from the traditional associations of male/superior soul ruling over female/inferior body, partners are enabled to practice relational power. Thus mutuality can be enhanced through Whitehead's conception of reciprocity and interdependence between body and soul.

An Embodied Spirituality of Mutuality for Christian Couples

Dare we suggest that the ongoing search that men and women alike have in our culture to . . . enrich their own experience of sexuality in all its dimension is a spiritual quest?[53]

Sexuality and spirituality are integrally connected as two aspects of the energetic experiences that compose human beings. "Yes" is the answer to the question posed by Penelope Washbourn in the earlier quotation: our search to enrich our experience of sexuality is a spiritual quest.

This chapter has examined the nature of the relationship between body and soul, and between sexuality and spirituality, so as to support the position that for Christian couples, understanding the body and sexuality to have positive roles in spiritual development enhances mutuality and repudiates violence against wives. The following three points elaborate the positive roles of the body and sexuality for spiritual development.

Body as Sacred

First, the body is sacred and not inferior to the soul. Following Julian's theology, the body is sacred because the body is co-substantial with the body of Jesus Christ; the body is the residence of the Divine because the body bears the image of God. To strike the body is to violate God's image, to assault the body of Christ. Thus in marriage, the bodies of both wife and husband are considered sacred, and there is no justification for the husband to beat his wife.

Building on the insights of Julian, Schleiermacher, and Whitehead, I propose that both body and soul are constituted by shared experiences in a relationship of reciprocity as body and soul alternately guide each other. As the body mediates experiences of the world and bodily sensations to the soul, the body provides wisdom to the soul. Since the body has this primary role in spiritual as well as physical development, the bodies of both husband and wife should be honored.

The key role of the body is also recognized for both wives and husbands because, following the anthropologies of Julian, Schleiermacher, Tillich, and Whitehead, gender is not assigned to either body or soul. The theological justification for the wife's subordination to her husband based on the wife's inferior body is rejected because the body is not inferior and woman is not associated with the body. In contradiction to the image of marriage as the union of a female body with a male soul or "head," the woman and the man are conceived as two complete human beings, each bringing a body and soul into partnership with each other to create a new relationship. They are not two halves searching for completion in another person.

This conception of wife and husband as two complete human beings negates the basis for the idea that the husband has ownership of the wife's body. Since the wife is not a body in need of a "head," the husband is not given ownership of his wife's body on the basis that he is her "head." And the husband has no authority to chastise or correct his wife as a "body" that needs to be disciplined. The wife has ownership of her body and is responsible for her actions just as the husband has ownership of his body and is responsible for his actions. As marriage partners, wife and husband choose to share their bodies and souls with each other. And because in a relational world we are changed by our relationships, the ongoing development of each one's body and soul will be deeply influenced by the other in the marital relationship. Yet each one retains ownership and authority for herself or himself in the relationship they are developing.

Acknowledging that the husband is not the head of his wife's body also repudiates the justification for the husband's control of his wife, a control that has sometimes been maintained with violence. A husband is held accountable for violence against his wife just as he is held accountable for violence against any other person—that is, he is prosecuted for assault and battery according to the laws of the state.

Complete Human Beings

Second, the belief that both wife and husband are complete human beings also has ramifications for the understanding of sexuality in this embodied spirituality of mutuality. Since both wife and husband are recognized as having bodies, they are both embodied, sexual beings. The husband's role in procreation is acknowledged, so that the wife is not associated with sexuality and procreation more than the husband. The wife is not considered to be created solely for the purpose of procreation or sexual service to the husband; thus the husband is not justified in using violence to coerce or control his wife's sexual expression. Just as wife and husband each retain control of her or his own body, wife and husband also retain the authority for her or his own sexuality. As both husband and wife act on their own authority, sexual intimacy in marriage can be a means of enhancing communication with each other and with God because each partner is acting without coercion from the other.

Following Tillich and Parker, sexuality can be a medium of experiencing God's presence and God's love for creation. Sexuality is freed from its inherent connection to sin because newborn human flesh is not corrupt. Rather, our bodies are the means of our first experience of the action of God in this world as we are miraculously created from other human beings.[54] Sexuality is integrally connected with spirituality because these are two aspects of the experiences that constitute human beings. Thus sexual intimacy in marriage is one means of experiencing God in the marriage partnership, and a husband's violent abuse of his wife to obtain intercourse is also an abuse of his relationship with God.

Spirituality, the Body, and Social Change

Third, spirituality can be experienced through the body as well as the soul. For example, one can experience relationship to God and other creatures through dance, sexual intimacy, or gardening, as well as through reading the Bible and prayer. As I have stated earlier, I define spirituality as the awareness of being in connection or relationship with God and with all creatures. This awareness can be nurtured, obstructed, or ignored by our personal choices as well as by our social context that influences how we choose to use our creative power.

When persons deny their spirituality, they lose awareness of their connection to God and creation. Without this awareness of connection, others may be treated as objects rather than subjects, and expressions of sexuality can become pornographic. For example, if one person is not aware that she is connected to another person because they constitute each other (following Whitehead's conception of the relationship between soul, body, and world as described above), she will probably not be aware that when she harms another person, she harms herself. Thus she can more easily exploit another person as an object for satisfying her desires, rather than recognizing the other person as another subject with desires similar to or different from her own. Susan Griffin names this connection between pornography and the denial of spirituality that reduces the other to an object: "The pornographer reduces a woman to a mere thing, to an entirely material object without a soul, who can only be 'loved' physically."[55]

Similarly in a battering relationship, the husband reduces the wife to an object in order to justify his violent behavior toward her. Pamela Cooper-White describes this process as the loss of relationship beginning with objectification and ending in legitimation of violence: "The abuser makes a critical shift in perspective, no longer seeing her [his wife] as a human being, equally precious as himself, but only as an object to be manipulated."[56] Like the pornographer, the violent husband reduces the woman from subject to object, denying her humanity. And in this process, both the pornographer and the violent husband deny their own humanity as well because their humanity is constituted by their relationship with the woman they have objectified.

Because spirituality or awareness of connection to others can be experienced through the body as well as the soul, one can also nurture or deny one's spirituality through how one satisfies bodily desires. Augustine rightly asserts that bodily desires are not inherently sinful, although one commits a sinful act if these desires are satisfied in ways that are harmful to self or others. However, Augustine's analysis of the relationship between sexual desire and rationality is faulty in a relational world. For Augustine, the problem with the human sexual drive is that it does not remain under the control of the rational will. Thus he creates a necessary opposition between the two and names all nonrational behavior (including sexual desire) as improper. Yet in a relational understanding of the self, this opposition is not inherent because human will is not separable from rational and nonrational thoughts or from feelings formed through bodily perceptions. Nonrational thoughts, feelings, and actions, such as intuitions or desires, have no necessary connection with sin. Augustine's emphasis on rationality as the standard for human behavior at all times ignores the role and value of intuition and desire in human experience. There can be occasions when nonrationality is necessary to inspire persons to move beyond stagnation to growth.

Thus, rather than labeling the expression of sexuality as sinful, we should value sexuality as a source of passionate energy needed to work against corporate evil in our nuclear age. Audre Lorde suggests the connection between suppressed energy and oppression: "In order to perpetuate itself, every oppression must corrupt or distort those various sources of power within the culture of the oppressed that can provide energy for change. For women, this has meant a suppression of the erotic as a considered source of power and information within our lives." Rather than being suppressed as sinful, the energy of sexual passion can be constructively channeled toward passionate action against sinful conditions in this world.[57]

Our passion, both spiritual and physical, draws us into acknowledging that we are connected to others. This is important because individuals cannot dismantle corporate structures. We must acknowledge that communities have created structures of exploitation, and therefore communities must work together to dismantle these structures and to create new ones of mutually empowering relationships. For example, our present knowledge regarding the pervasiveness and magnitude of violence against wives compels us to repudiate the power imbalance in the traditionally structured roles of wife and husband.

One step toward creating a structure of mutual empowerment for couples is to encourage partners to honor their partner's body and soul, as well as their own body and soul, as a means of experiencing relatedness to God and to each other. By acknowledging that God is present in both the body and soul of the partner, couples can develop a spirituality that unites their sexual and spiritual passion to work for social change.

CHAPTER SIX

Marriage and Social Change

Love does not consist in gazing at each other, but in looking outward together in the same direction.

Antoine de Saint-Exupéry[1]

Society would have to be transfigured by the glimpse of a new type of social personality, a new humanity appropriate to a new earth.

Rosemary Radford Ruether[2]

arriage as mutual empowerment and redemption through intimacy has implications for developing new social personalities for wives and husbands to facilitate social change, the transfiguration of society called for by Ruether in the epigraph above. Other scholars have discussed how marriage and the family unit can provide stability during times of great social upheaval, for example, during the collapse of the feudal system in the Reformation period of sixteenth-century Europe.[3] In contrast,

I hold that social change can be promoted by reimagining the institution of Christian marriage from predetermined, hierarchical roles to a fluid and flexible committed relationship of mutual empowerment that facilitates redemption through intimacy.[4] Because marriage is one of the foundational institutions of society, the new paradigm of marriage as mutual empowerment has profound implications for the larger society. This chapter examines these implications to illuminate the public aspect of marriage, not the privatization of marriage as a relationship between just two people.

The preceding chapters have described how couples can facilitate redemption in their intimate partnerships and in their communities by practicing relational power as follows. Based on the Whiteheadian principle that our personal identity is constituted by our relationships, our intimate partner relationships are therefore one of our greatest opportunities both for sin and for redemption. Partners can experience redemptive intimacy because the practice of relational power creates the "true good" that can emerge only in mutual relationships. Furthermore, our capacity for intimacy is enhanced when we embrace an understanding of God that conceives God as in the process of becoming through God's interactions with the world. As we experience the intimacy of cocreating with God by participating in forming the divine nature, we can be encouraged to risk the intimacy of cocreating mutuality with a human partner. Intimacy is also enhanced through the conception of reciprocity in the relationship between body and soul in which the body has a positive role in spiritual development and sexual intimacy can be a means of experiencing God's presence and love. Freed from the traditional associations of male/superior soul ruling over female/inferior body, partners are enabled to practice relational power.

These alternative conceptions of God and power, sin and redemption, body and soul, and sexuality and spirituality offer a theological ideal of intimate partner relationships that are free of hierarchical gender associations and violence and are deeply mutual in the sharing of power. This theological ideal can support Christians working for social change in three areas: restoring right relationships in society, reducing violence against women, and responding to the current public marriage debate by advocating one Christian sexual ethic for all intimate partners.

Restoring Right Relationships

The new paradigm of marriage as mutual empowerment provides a model for restoring right relationship in the order of creation not only between wives and husbands, but also between women and men and between groups of humans in general. Just as this paradigm addresses issues of power between husbands and wives, the implications of this position also critique power imbalances in the larger social structure.

One traditional theological justification for the subordination of wives to husbands was the belief that all women as daughters of Eve were to be punished due to Eve's sin. However, the husband's rule over the wife (Gen. 3:16) is a result of sin, not God's original intention for creation. Therefore, Christians today should be working to create marriage relationships that restore God's original intention rather than perpetuate the distortion of power caused by sin. And if all women are daughters of Eve (and all men are sons of Adam), then God's intention for mutuality between Eve and Adam also applies to the relationships between all women and men.

The distortion of God's intention for mutuality between women and men has been justified by theological understandings of sexuality that have been used to serve the interests of those in power. For example, Augustine's anthropology of male/soul as superior to female/body and his understanding of female sexuality as more tainted with sin due to the female's role in procreation functioned well for ruling male elites. Furthermore, Augustine, Luther, and Freud understood sin or the human condition as the struggle of the rational will or ego over and against the sexual drive. Sexual desire was labeled irrational, creating a harmful hierarchy within individuals, which then could be used to justify oppressive hierarchies in society. The group in power labeled other groups as irrational or more prone to acting out sexual desires, and the control of these groups was justified. For example, women were labeled irrational and associated with sexuality; thus women needed to be controlled, even through the use of violence.

The argument that God's intention is for mutuality between males and females can also be applied to the relationships between humans in general because this position challenges traditional theologies that justified keeping some groups of women and men subordinated. For example, in Luther's day the hierarchical feudal system was accepted as the proper order of creation ordained by God. The explanation of humanity's relationship to God as one of servants to ruler justified those in power who ruled over persons deemed inferior due to their race or economic status. Today, feminist, womanist, and other liberation theologians are questioning the hierarchical corporate structures that have facilitated sins of violence and other forms of oppression. We are claiming that humans, not God, have created the societal structures that promote sexism, racism, and militarism. Original sin can be more accurately named as contextual sin because social structures of oppression, rather than corrupt natures, are our inheritance from previous generations. I join with others who are challenging these structures by proposing a model of mutual empowerment for arranging relationships among humans and God. In a relational world, humans are recognized as cocreators with God, rather than servants of a sacred ruler. A model of mutual empowerment considers females and males as equally responsible and capable of acting as moral agents in the community of creation. This model challenges psychological theories such as Freud's that conceive females as incapable of mature moral development. Therefore, Christians should be working to dismantle the social structures that perpetuate subordination based on gender, race, or class in order to restore the order of creation that God intended.

Repudiating Violence against Women

By proposing alternative understandings of God, power, sin, body, and sexuality that repudiate violence against wives in Christian marriage, this paradigm of marriage provides a theological basis for Christian communities to work against other forms of violence, particularly violence against women. The traditional disciplinary model of marriage is transformed to a model of mutual empowerment by dismantling the traditional hierarchy that legitimated the wife's subordination and the husband's use of violence to enforce this subordination. In a marriage partnership of mutual empowerment, the wife and husband are conceived as two complete human beings choosing to create a nonhierarchical relationship free of violence.

The transformation of marriage from a disciplinary relationship to one of mutual empowerment is based in the theological understanding that the female body, as well as the male body, bears the image of God. Like the male body, the female body is sacred and a source of wisdom for the soul, and sexual intimacy can be a means of experiencing God's presence and love. By extension, all female bodies should be respected and not subject to any form of violence, including not only physical and sexual assault, but also psychological abuse. Thus Christians should be actively supporting local community groups who are working to reduce violence against women, for example, rape crisis hotlines, domestic violence shelters, and rehabilitation education programs for perpetrators. As Marie M. Fortune has written, "Victims don't need platitudes. They need real acts of mercy, compassion, hospitality and justice. Abusers don't need sympathy. They need someone who cares enough to hold them accountable and help bring them to repentance."[5] By forming alliances with social service organizations, Christian groups can be more effective in their efforts to minister to women and men caught in violent relationships.[6]

When working to reduce violence against women, addressing issues of economic justice is also important because women can be trapped in violent relationships due to economic dependency. Discrimination against women in the workplace can prevent women from earning salaries that enable them to support themselves and their children.[7] Christian church groups can be proactive by supporting companies who comply with laws mandating workplace environments free of sexual harassment and equal treatment of women in salaries and promotion.

Addressing popular definitions of masculinity is another important aspect in working to reduce violence against women. Christian denominations should develop church school curricula and catechetical materials that present countercultural definitions of masculinity, definitions that do not include proving one's manhood through power over others and violence. For example, educational materials could focus on interpretations of Jesus as a man who used nonviolent methods to oppose unjust social structures of his time.[8] Jesus could also be portrayed as a man who, according to many of the Gospel stories, treated women as equals and worthy of respect, even women who had violated the laws governing sexual behavior and were thus considered deserving of social condemnation or death by violent means.[9]

A Christian Sexual Ethic

The new paradigm of marriage as mutual empowerment has implications for Christians working to resolve the current public marriage debate by proposing a Christian sexual ethic for both heterosexual and homosexual couples in a relational world. This ethic is based in the theology developed in this book regarding God's nature and the relationship between God and human sexual love.

Understandings of God in a relational world challenge the image of an apathetic, impassible Being. God is named as Divine Eros, Lover, Friend, and power in mutual relation. God's nature develops as God relates to creation, a creation in the process of being constituted by interdependent relationships. Thus human possibilities for intimacy are enhanced as humans relate to God and to creation. Body and soul are composed of shared experiences as the human is continually coming into being in community with God and creation, and body and soul develop in a mutually dependent relationship as each alternately guides the other. The traditional Western hierarchical dualism between body and soul is transformed into reciprocity so that the wisdom of the body and the wisdom of the soul develop in proportion to each other.

With these foundational understandings of God, body, and soul, human sexuality is both an opportunity for God to express God's own creative nature and a primary, powerful source for human creativity. As humans have the freedom to express creativity through sexual intimacy, our sexuality has enormous potential for good and evil, for sin and redemption. Precisely because sexuality is a central element in the developing of human life and God's life, sexual expression should be ordered toward the good of the fullest possibilities for all in the community.[10] Humans can best fulfill our possibilities for participating in Divine Love and for loving ourselves and others when our sexual love is expressed in committed, mutually empowering partnerships that sustain the community. This Christian sexual ethical provides an ideal for gay and lesbian couples as well as for heterosexual couples before and during marriage.

This ideal offers a vision of God, intimate partnerships, and community in which the richest possibilities for both love and justice can be fulfilled, because in a relational world, couples not only influence the becoming of each other for good or evil; they also influence the becoming of their community. Suchocki describes this dynamic influence: "The value of communities as well as the value of individuals is to be judged finally not simply in terms of self-significance, but in terms of significance for others in the increasingly wider communities of the world and universe."[11] Therefore, one criterion for determining sanctioned partnerships in our society is not the gender of the two persons, but rather the quality of partner relationships that will enable the greatest development of good for the partners and in the community. In agreement with Bernard Loomer, I have argued that the "true good" can only emerge through the practice of relational power in deeply mutual relationships. With relational power as our criterion, we could simultaneously strive toward mutual empowerment in our intimate partnerships and work to change social structures that perpetuate violence and oppression through unilateral power.

The continued practice of unilateral power will facilitate the destruction of all of us in our ecologically fragile nuclear age, ravaged by war and threats of war. Imagine a world in which community and national leaders use their power to develop persuasive strategies of peace, rather than to develop increasingly effective coercive weapons of destruction. In this world, power will be shared as marriage relationships and relationships between all persons are restored to the mutuality God intended in the order of creation, and violence against women and men will be

NOTES

Preface

1. Stephanie Coontz, *Marriage, a History: From Obedience to Intimacy, or How Love Conquered Marriage* (New York: Penguin Books, 2006), 311.
2. Dalma Heyn, *Marriage Shock: The Transformation of Women into Wives* (New York: Villard Books, 1997), 18.
3. Rose M. Kreider, *Census Bureau: Number, Timing and Duration of Marriages and Divorces, 2001* (Washington, D.C.: U.S. Census Bureau, Current Population Reports, 2005), 70–97, http://www.census.gov/prod/2005pubs/p70–97.pdf (December 3, 2007).
4. "Bureau of Justice Statistics Crime Data Brief," *Intimate Partner Violence, 1993–2001* (February 2003), cited in "Domestic Violence Is a Serious, Widespread Social Problem in America: The Facts," 2005, http://endabuse.org/resources/facts/ (January 9, 2005).
5. L. Heise and C. Garcia-Moreno, "Violence by Intimate Partners," *World Report on Violence and Health* (Geneva: World Health Organization, 2002), cited in "Intimate Partner Violence: Fact Sheet," National Center for Injury Prevention and Control, 2004, http://www.cdc.gov/ncipc/factsheets/ipvfacts.htm (January 9, 2005).
6. For example, see John Witte Jr., M. Christian Green, and Amy Wheeler, eds., *The Equal-Regard Family and Its Friendly Critics: Don Browning and the Practical Theological Ethics of the Family* (Grand Rapids: Eerdmans, 2007); Don S. Browning, Bonnie J. Miller-McLemore, Pamela D. Couture,

K. Brynolf Lyon, and Robert M. Franklin, *From Culture Wars to Common Ground: Religion and the American Family Debate*, 2nd ed. (Louisville, Ky.: Westminster John Knox, 2000); Rosemary Radford Ruether, *Christianity and the Making of the Modern Family* (Boston: Beacon, 2000); Anne Carr and Mary Stewart Van Leeuwen, eds., *Religion, Feminism, and the Family* (Louisville, Ky.: Westminster John Knox, 1996); Don S. Browning, *Marriage and Modernization: How Globalization Threatens Marriage and What to Do about It* (Grand Rapids: Eerdmans, 2003); Carrie A. Miles, *The Redemption of Love: Rescuing Marriage and Sexuality from the Economics of a Fallen World* (Grand Rapids: Brazos, 2006); Kirean Scott and Michael Warren, eds., *Perspectives on Marriage: A Reader*, 3rd ed. (New York: Oxford University Press, 2007); and Katherine Anderson, Don Browning, and Brian Boyer, eds., *Marriage: Just a Piece of Paper?* (Grand Rapids: Eerdmans, 2002).

Chapter 1 Rethinking Power

1. Adrian Thatcher, *Marriage after Modernity: Christian Marriage in Postmodern Times* (New York: New York University Press, 1999), 223.

2. "What's Love Got to Do with It?" by Terry Britten and Graham Lyle, © 1984 by Myaxe Music Ltd & Good Single Music, Ltd. Myaxe Music Ltd. Published in U.S.A. by Chappell & Co., Inc. International Copyright Secured. All rights reserved. Used by permission.

3. L. Heise and C. Garcia-Moreno, "Violence by Intimate Partners," *World Report on Violence and Health* (Geneva: World Health Organization, 2002), cited in "Intimate Partner Violence: Fact Sheet," National Center for Injury Prevention and Control, 2004, http://www.cdc.gov/ncipc/factsheets/ipvfacts.htm (June 5, 2008; inactive).

4. From "Battering Statistics," compiled in October 1996 by the Los Angeles Commission on Assaults against Women, 605 West Olympic Boulevard, Suite 400, Los Angeles, CA 90015.

5. *Health Concerns across a Woman's Lifespan: 1998 Survey of Women's Health* (The Commonwealth Fund, May 1999),

cited in "Domestic Violence Is a Serious, Widespread Social Problem in America: The Facts," 2005, http://endabuse.org/resources/facts/ (January 9, 2005).

6. Center for Family and Demographic Research at Bowling Green State University, "Divorce and Remarriage," http://www.bgsu.edu/organizations/cfdr/ (June 5, 2008).

7. Dalma Heyn, *Marriage Shock: The Transformation of Women into Wives* (New York: Villard Books, 1997), 18. I thank Grace Jones Moore for bringing this book to my attention.

8. *Merriam-Webster's Online Dictionary*, s.v. "intimate," http://www.merriam-webster.com/dictionary/intimate (June 5, 2008).

9. For a discussion of *pater familias*, see Sarah B. Pomeroy, *Goddesses, Whores, Wives, and Slaves: Women in Classical Antiquity* (New York: Schocken Books, 1975), 150–51. Only those few women who became Vestal Virgins were automatically exempt from the power of the *pater familias*.

10. For a discussion of the practice of the "Rule of Thumb," see Lawrence Stone, *The Family, Sex and Marriage in England, 1500–1899* (New York: Harper & Row, 1977), 326.

11. Joy M. K. Bussert, *Battered Women: From a Theology of Suffering to an Ethic of Empowerment* (New York: Lutheran Church in America, 1986), 12.

12. Cited in Stephanie Coontz, *Marriage, a History: From Obedience to Intimacy, or How Love Conquered Marriage* (New York: Penguin Books, 2006), 141.

13. Ibid.

14. Ibid., 241.

15. Ibid.

16. See Barbara Corrado Pope, "Angels in the Devil's Workshop: Leisured and Charitable Women in Nineteenth-Century England and France," in *Becoming Visible: Women in European History*, ed. Renate Bridenthal and Claudia Koonz (Boston: Houghton Mifflin, 1977), 309.

17. Stephanie Coontz, "The Heterosexual Revolution," *New York Times*, July 5, 2005, http://www.nytimes.com/2005/07/05/opinion/05coontz.html?_r=1&ei=50&oref=slogin (June 5, 2008; subscription).

18. The relationship between the Christian tradition and violence against wives is cogently described by Rosemary

Radford Ruether in her article "The Western Religious Tradition and Violence against Women in the Home," in *Christianity, Patriarchy, and Abuse: A Feminist Critique*, ed. Joanne Carlson Brown and Carole R. Bohn (Cleveland: Pilgrim, 1989), 31–41.

19. Cited in Julia O'Faolain and Lauro Martines, eds., *Not in God's Image* (New York: Harper & Row, 1973), 177.

20. Glenda Kaufman Kantor and Jana L. Jasinski, "Dynamics and Risk Factors in Partner Violence," in *Partner Violence: A Comprehensive Review of 20 Years of Research*, ed. Jana L. Jasinski and Linda M. Williams (Thousand Oaks, Calif.: Sage, 1998), 5.

21. Heise and Garcia-Moreno, "Violence by Intimate Partners."

22. Michele Harway and James M. O'Neil, eds. *What Causes Men's Violence against Women?* (Thousand Oaks, Calif.: Sage, 1999), 209.

23. James M. O'Neil and Rodney A. Nadeau, "Men's Gender-Role Conflict, Defense Mechanisms, and Self-Protective Defensive Strategies: Explaining Men's Violence against Women from a Gender-Role Socialization Perspective," in Harway and O'Neil, *What Causes Men's Violence*, 103.

24. Harway and O'Neil, *What Causes Men's Violence*, 240.

25. Roberta L. Nutt, "Women's Gender-Role Socialization, Gender-Role Conflict, and Abuse: A Review of Predisposing Factors," in Harway and O'Neil, *What Causes Men's Violence*, 131–132.

26. Bernard Loomer, "Two Conceptions of Power," *Process Studies* 6, no. 1 (1976). Brock actually uses the term "erotic power." However, she defines erotic power as "the fundamental power of existence-as-a-relational-process." See Rita Nakashima Brock, *Journeys by Heart: A Christology of Erotic Power* (New York: Crossroad, 1991), 41. For another discussion of alternative forms of power, see Pamela Cooper-White, *The Cry of Tamar: Violence against Women and the Church's Response* (Minneapolis: Fortress Press, 1995), 30–40.

27. Loomer, "Two Conceptions of Power," 17.

28. Ibid., 8.

29. Ibid., 22.
30. Brock, *Journeys by Heart*, 34.
31. Loomer, "Two Conceptions of Power," 19.
32. Brock, *Journeys by Heart*, 32.
33. O'Neil and Nadeau, "Men's Gender-Role Conflict," 103.
34. Heyn, *Marriage Shock*, 186–87.
35. Robert M. Sapolsky, "Testosterone Rules," in *The Gendered Society Reader*, 2nd ed., ed. Michael S. Kimmel with Amy Aronson (New York: Oxford University Press, 2004), 26–32.
36. Loomer, "Two Conceptions of Power," 18.
37. Ibid.
38. *Merriam-Webster's Online Dictionary*, s.v. "redeem," http://www.merriam-webster.com/dictionary/redeem (June 5, 2008).
39. Phyllis Trible, "Genesis 2–3 Reread," in *Womanspirit Rising: A Feminist Reader in Religion*, ed. Carol P. Christ and Judith Plaskow (San Francisco: Harper & Row, 1979), 75. Trible's thesis is that Genesis 2–3 describes humans as "creatures of equality and mutuality" who became "creatures of oppression" due to sin. The text calls for males and females to repent and return to their original state. See also Gilbert Bilezikian, *Beyond Sex Roles: What the Bible Says about a Woman's Place in Church and Family*, 3rd ed. (Grand Rapids: Baker Academic, 2006), 17–43. For a summary of the current debate among evangelicals and feminists about how Genesis 1–2 should be interpreted, see William H. Jennings, *Storms over Genesis: Biblical Battleground in America's Wars of Religion* (Minneapolis: Fortress Press, 2007), 25–50.
40. Loomer, "Two Conceptions of Power," 19.
41. Ibid., 23.
42. Ibid., 19.
43. Ibid., 20–21.
44. Henry Nelson Wieman, *The Source of Human Good* (Carbondale, Ill.: Southern Illinois University Press, 1946), 17, 19.
45. Ibid., 236.
46. Ibid., 242.

47. Ibid., 238.

48. Alfred North Whitehead, "Mathematics and the Good," in *The Philosophy of Alfred North Whitehead*, ed. Paul Arthur Schilpp (LaSalle: Open Court, 1941), 670.

49. Loomer, "Two Conceptions of Power," 20.

50. Brock, *Journeys by Heart*, 34.

51. Marjorie Hewitt Suchocki, *God, Christ, Church: A Practical Guide to Process Theology* (New York: Crossroad, 1988), 22.

52. Loomer, "Two Conceptions of Power," 26.

53. For a lively discussion of whether or not Christianity teaches male headship, see David Blankenhorn, Don Browning, and Mary Stewart Van Leeuwen, eds., *Does Christianity Teach Male Headship? The Equal-Regard Marriage and Its Critics* (Grand Rapids: Eerdmans, 2004).

54. Clarice J. Martin, "The *Haustafeln* (Household Codes) in African American Biblical Interpretation: 'Free Slaves' and 'Subordinate Women,'" in *Stony the Road We Trod: African American Biblical Interpretation*, ed. Cain Hope Felder (Minneapolis: Fortress Press, 1991), 212–13. See also "Ephesians," "Colossians," and "1 Peter," in Carol A. Newsom and Sharon H. Ringe, *The Women's Bible Commentary* (Louisville, Ky.: Westminster John Knox, 1992), 338–42, 346–48, and 370–72.

55. Elisabeth Schüssler Fiorenza, *In Memory of Her: A Feminist Theological Reconstruction of Christian Origins* (New York: Crossroad, 1983), 140–51, 208–18. See also Rosemary Radford Ruether, *Christianity and the Making of the Modern Family* (Boston: Beacon, 2000).

56. Martin, "The *Haustafeln*," 213.

57. Catherine Clark Kroeger, "Let's Look Again at the Biblical Concept of Submission," in *Violence against Women and Children: A Christian Theological Sourcebook*, ed. Carol J. Adams and Marie M. Fortune (New York: Continuum, 1995), 139.

58. Ibid, 139.

59. Ibid., 140.

60. Ibid.

61. Martin, "The *Haustafeln*," 220.

Chapter 2 God

1. *Catholic News Service*, "Catholic Church Workers Must Explain Marriage Reflects God's Love, Pope Says," May 20, 2007, http://www.catholic.org/printer_friendly.php?id =24154&section=Cathcom (June 5, 2008; inactive).

2. Janet Edwards, "Midweek Perspectives: I Plead Innocent: Same-Sex Marriages Can Reflect God's Covenant with Creation, Too," *Post-Gazette.com: A Service of the Pittsburgh Post-Gazette*, October 4, 2006, http://www.post-gazette.com/pg/pp/06277/727109.stm (June 2008; inactive).

3. Alfred North Whitehead, *Process and Reality*, corrected edition, ed. David Ray Griffin and Donald W. Sherburne (New York: Free Press, 1978 [1929]), 351.

4. Van A. Harvey, *A Handbook of Theological Terms*, s.v. "impassible" (New York: Macmillan, 1964), 129.

5. I am indebted to Barbara Keiller for stimulating my imagination and thinking about intimacy and the Whiteheadian notion of God. See Keiller, "A Process Relational Vision of God Enhances Our Capacity for Intimacy with Each Other and with the Cosmos," *Creative Transformation* 1, no. 1 (1991): 8–11.

6. For another discussion of God from a relational worldview, see Catherine Keller's provocative theology in *On the Mystery: Discerning Divinity in Process* (Minneapolis: Fortress Press, 2008). For a strong analysis of the strengths and weaknesses of the view of God as relational, see Flora A. Keshgegian, *God Reflected: Metaphors for Life* (Minneapolis: Fortress Press, 2008), 142–46.

7. Sallie McFague, *Models of God: Theology for an Ecological, Nuclear Age* (Philadelphia: Fortress Press, 1987), 92.

8. Rosemary Radford Ruether, "The Western Religious Tradition and Violence against Women in the Home," in *Christianity, Patriarchy, and Abuse: A Feminist Critique*, ed. Joanne Carlson Brown and Carole R. Bohn (Cleveland: Pilgrim, 1989), 31.

9. Ibid., 33.

10. This statement is found on the official Web site of the Southern Baptist Convention, under the section entitled "Basic Beliefs." See http://www.sbc.net/aboutus/basicbeliefs.asp

(June 5, 2008). For further comments on the 1998 resolution, see Kenneth L. Woodward, "Using the Bully Pulpit?" *Newsweek*, June 22, 1998, 69. Online at http://www.newsweek.com/id/92884?tid=relatedcl (June 5, 2008).

11. Augustine, *On the Trinity*, XXII, in *A Select Library of Nicene and Post-Nicene Fathers of the Christian Church*, vol. 3, ed. Philip Schaff, trans. Arthur West Haddan (Grand Rapids: Eerdmans, 1956), 159.

12. Harvey, *Handbook*, s.v. "God," 106.

13. Ibid., 129.

14. See Herbert Haag et al., *Great Couples of the Bible*, trans. Brian McNeil (Minneapolis: Fortress Press, 2006).

15. Kristen E. Kvam, Linda S. Schearing, and Valarie H. Ziegler, eds., *Eve and Adam: Jewish, Christian, and Muslim Readings on Genesis and Gender* (Bloomington: Indiana University Press, 1999), back cover.

16. Mignon R. Jacobs, *Gender, Power, and Persuasion: The Genesis Narratives and Contemporary Portraits* (Grand Rapids: Baker Academic, 2007), 42.

17. For a compelling analysis of God's intervention from the perspective of Hagar, see Delores S. Williams, *Sisters in the Wilderness: The Challenge of Womanist God-Talk* (Maryknoll, N.Y.: Orbis Books, 1993), 15–33.

18. Elisabeth Schüssler Fiorenza, *In Memory of Her: A Feminist Theological Reconstruction of Christian Origins* (New York: Crossroad, 1983), 172.

19. For a brief defense of why "Junia" is the correct name in Romans 16:7, see Elisabeth Schüssler Fiorenza, "Women in the Early Christian Movement," in *Womanspirit Rising: A Feminist Reader in Religion*, ed. Carol P. Christ and Judith Plaskow (New York: HarperSanFrancisco, 1992), 90.

20. In short, Whitehead's God is an actuality that originates outside of time and is the source of novelty or possibilities and order for all beings in the world. The form of God's being is a reverse image of the world. God is not a "person" because persons exist in time and are only one aspect of creation. God is more than a person. However, Whitehead attributes personal qualities to God such as responsive love, persuasive power, wisdom, infinite patience, and

companionship. For further discussions of Whitehead's God, see Whitehead, *Process and Reality*, 342–51; Donald W. Sherburne, ed., *A Key to Whitehead's Process and Reality* (Chicago: University of Chicago Press, 1966); John B. Cobb Jr. and David Ray Griffin, *Process Theology: An Introductory Exposition* (Philadelphia: Westminster, 1976); and Marjorie Hewitt Suchocki, *God Christ Church: A Practical Guide to Process Theology* (New York: Crossroad, 1988).

21. Whitehead, *Process and Reality*, 108, 343.
22. God's primordial nature is described as "creative love" in Cobb and Griffin, *Process Theology*, 48–52.
23. Alfred North Whitehead, *Adventures of Ideas* (New York: Free Press, 1961 [1933]), 277.
24. Ibid.
25. Whitehead, *Process and Reality*, 345.
26. Ibid., 12.
27. Ibid., 345.
28. Ibid.
29. Ibid., 346.
30. Ibid., 351.
31. Cobb and Griffin, *Process Theology*, 48.
32. Whitehead, *Process and Reality*, 342.
33. Ibid., 343.
34. Ibid., 346.
35. McFague, *Models of God*, 128–29.
36. Ibid., 130.
37. Ibid., 128.
38. Ibid., 69–87.
39. Ibid., 130.
40. Ibid., 129.
41. Ibid., 134.
42. Ibid.
43. Ibid., 152.
44. *Oxford Student's Dictionary*, 1st ed., s.v. "intimacy."
45. McFague, *Models of God*, 162.
46. Ibid., 164.
47. Ibid., 163. The "classical roots" are Aristotle's writings about friendship in *Ethics*.
48. Ibid.

49. Ibid.
50. Ibid., 178.
51. *Oxford*, s.v. "companion."
52. Ibid., 168.
53. Ibid., 165.
54. Ibid., 171.
55. Carter Heyward, *Touching Our Strength: The Erotic as Power and the Love of God* (San Francisco: Harper & Row, 1989), 188.
56. Ibid., 46.
57. Ibid., 23.
58. Ibid.
59. Ibid., 23–24. Heyward acknowledges that the Deity is neither female nor male. However, Heyward sometimes uses "She" to affirm the sacred power of women and to indicate that her concept of God includes more characteristics than the male God of dominant Christianity. See footnote on page 163 of *Touching Our Strength*.
60. Ibid., 99.
61. Ibid., 188–89.
62. Ibid., 189.
63. Ibid., 187.
64. Ibid., 99.
65. Ibid., 102.
66. Ibid., 91.
67. Ibid., 191.
68. Ibid.
69. Ibid., 96.
70. Ibid., 104.
71. Ibid., 105.
72. Ibid., 107.
73. Ibid., 104.
74. This view is illustrated in a poster from the suffrage movement in Britain (c. 1911–1912). Mr. and Mrs. John Bull are walking together as she holds the hand of a young child. Mr. Bull is holding an umbrella labeled "The Vote" so that the umbrella covers only his head. Mr. Bull says, "My umbrella protects us all!" Mrs. Bull replies, "No it does not, John. I

must have one of my own" (reprinted as postcard no. 27, Museum of London, 1986).

75. I am indebted to Jon Berkedal for bringing this point to my attention.
76. Heyward, *Touching Our Strength*, 34.
77. Ibid., 105.
78. Ibid., 106.
79. Ibid., 34.
80. McFague, *Models of God*, 19.

Chapter 3 A Legacy of Female Subordination

1. *Purple Pew News*, "(Gay) Marriage Counseling Needed for Anglican-Episcopal Church," February 20, 2007, http://purplepew.org/news/religion/20070220/gay-marriage-counseling-needed-for-anglican-episcopal-church (May 31, 2008).
2. Randy Rasmussen, quoted in Bob Ellis, "Nothing Wrong with Abortion Petition in Church," *Dakota Voice*, March 10, 2008, http://www.dakotavoice.com/2008/03/rasmussen-nothing-wrong-with-abortion.html (May 31, 2008).
3. Marie M. Fortune, "Sexual Abuse by Priests: An Institutional Crisis in the Catholic Church," in "Clergy Sexual Abuse: Theological and Gender Perspectives," *Faith Trust Institute*, http://www.faithtrustinstitute.org/downloads/aar_panel.pdf (May 31, 2008).
4. I am indebted to Mary Elizabeth Moore and Karen Jo Torjesen for their encouragement and careful critique of portions of chapters 3, 4, and 5 in an earlier draft.
5. Elaine M. Pagels, "The Politics of Paradise: Augustine's Exegesis of Genesis 1–3 versus That of John Chrysostom," *Harvard Theological Review* 78 (January–April 1985): 83.
6. Rather than following Pagels in using "sexual desire," I have chosen to use the term "uncontrolled sexual desire" because, as I demonstrate, the "sin" of sexual desire is that it is not under the control of the rational mind or soul.
7. Rosemary Radford Ruether, "Virginal Feminism in the Fathers of the Church," in *Religion and Sexism: Images of*

Women in Jewish and Christian Traditions, ed. Rosemary Radford Ruether (New York: Simon & Schuster, 1974), 158–59. For discussions of how virginity functioned for women in the early centuries of the Christian church, see Margaret R. Miles, "'Becoming Male': Women Martyrs and Ascetics," in *Carnal Knowing: Female Nakedness and Religious Meaning in the Christian West* (Boston: Beacon, 1989), 53–77; Elaine Pagels, "The 'Paradise of Virginity' Regained," in *Adam, Eve, and the Serpent* (New York: Vintage Books, 1989), 78–97; and Rosemary Radford Ruether, "Mothers of the Church: Ascetic Women in the Late Patristic Age," in *Women of Spirit: Female Leadership in the Jewish and Christian Traditions* (New York: Simon & Schuster, 1979), 72–98.

8. Augustine, "To Ecdicia," *Saint Augustine: Letters,* no. 262, in *The Fathers of the Church,* vol. 32, ed. Roy Joseph Deferrari, trans. Wilfrid Parsons (New York: Fathers of the Church, 1956), V, 261–69.

9. Elizabeth A. Clark, "Theory and Practice in Late Ancient Asceticism: Jerome, Chrysostom, and Augustine," *Journal of Feminist Studies in Religion* 5, no. 2 (1989): 45.

10. Augustine, *The Literal Meaning of Genesis,* in *Ancient Christian Writers,* vol. 42, ed. Johannes Quasten, Walter J. Burghardt, and Thomas Comerford Lawler, trans. John Hammond Taylor (New York: Newman, 1982), VI, 182–85.

11. Augustine, *Genesis,* IX, 75.

12. Karen Jo Torjesen, *When Women Were Priests: Women's Leadership in the Early Church and the Scandal of Their Subordination in the Rise of Christianity* (San Francisco: HarperSanFrancisco, 1993), 221, 223.

13. Ibid., 181.

14. Ibid., 115.

15. Ibid., 137.

16. Ibid., 186. Ironically, "Behind Closed Doors" is the title of a booklet published by House of Ruth, Inc., a domestic violence shelter in Claremont, California, that states: "Until recently, domestic violence was viewed as a family problem that existed 'Behind Closed Doors.'"

17. I am suggesting a connection between the designation of silence and obedience as female virtues in classical Greece and the behavior of contemporary battered wives who submit to their husbands' violence. For one discussion of how the ideals of silence and obedience influenced women in the intervening centuries, see Suzanne W. Hull, *Chaste, Silent, and Obedient: English Books for Women, 1475–1640* (San Marino, Calif.: Huntington Library, 1982).

18. For example, "In 1981 Duluth [Minnesota] was the first U.S. city to institute mandatory arrests in domestic disputes. Since then about half the states have done the same, which means that even if a victim does not wish to press charges, the police are obliged to make an arrest if they see evidence of abuse." Nancy Gibbs, " 'Til Death Do Us Part," *Time*, January 18, 1993, 45.

19. Augustine, *On the Trinity*, in *A Select Library of Nicene and Post-Nicene Fathers of the Christian Church*, vol. 3, ed. Philip Schaff, trans. Arthur West Haddan (Grand Rapids: Eerdmans, 1956), XII, 160.

20. Recent scholars have debated how Augustine's writings support and/or deny the equality of females and males. See Kari Elisabeth Borresen, *Subordination and Equivalence* (Washington, D.C.: University Press of America, 1981); Maryanne Cline Horowitz, "The Image of God in Man—Is Woman Included?" *Harvard Theological Review* 72 (1979): 175–206; and Cornelia W. Wolfskeel, "Some Remarks with Regard to Augustine's Conception of Man as the Image of God," *Vigiliae Christianae* 30 (1976): 63–71.

21. Augustine, *Trinity*, 159.

22. Ibid.

23. Ibid.

24. Ibid., 160.

25. Quoted in Del Martin, *Battered Wives* (San Francisco: Glide, 1976), 84.

26. Augustine, *Commentary on the Lord's Sermon on the Mount*, in *The Fathers of the Church*, vol. 11, ed. Roy Joseph Deferrari, trans. Denis J. Kavanagh (New York: Fathers of the Church, 1951), 61–62.

27. Augustine, *Confessions*, trans. R. S. Pine-Coffin (London: Penguin Books, 1961), IX, 195.

28. Ruether, "Virginal Feminism," 165.

29. Ibid.

30. Ibid. Torjesen notes: "By the first and second centuries of the common era, a [Roman] woman could escape both the father's *potestas* [power] and the husband's *manus* [hand] by placing herself under the guardianship of a nonfamilial 'tutor,' whom she might even choose herself." Torjesen, *When Women Were Priests*, 61.

31. Women are named the "'appropriate' victims of 'marital' violence" by Emerson and Russell Dobash as they explore how "legal, historical, literary, and religious writings" throughout Western history almost always conceive the role of women as defined only by women's personal relationships to men. Dobash and Dobash, *Violence against Wives: A Case against Patriarchy* (New York: Free Press, 1979), 32.

32. For an alternative view, see Jane Dempsey Douglas, "Women and the Continental Reformation," in *Religion and Sexism: Images of Woman in the Jewish and Christian Traditions*, ed. Rosemary Radford Ruether (New York: Simon & Schuster, 1974), 292–318.

33. Karen Armstrong notes this change in the theological construction of woman's nature: "It was a new twist to the Eve myth. Instead of powerfully leading men to their spiritual doom, the new Protestant Eve is not exactly wicked; she is just so weak and so spiritually enfeebled that she hasn't a hope of salvation unless guided by her husband." Armstrong, *The Gospel according to Woman: Christianity's Creation of the Sex War in the West* (Garden City, N.Y.: Anchor/Doubleday, 1986), 312.

34. Martin Luther, *Lectures on Genesis*, in *Luther's Works*, vol. 1, ed. Jaroslav Pelikan, trans. George V. Schick (St. Louis, Mo.: Concordia, 1958 [1535–45]), 159.

35. Martin Luther, *The Freedom of a Christian*, in *Three Treatises*, trans. W. A. Lambert, rev. Harold J. Grimm (Philadelphia: Fortress Press, 1970 [1520]), 286.

36. Ibid., 287.

37. Luther, *Genesis*, 269–70.
38. Martin Luther, *The Babylonian Captivity of the Church*, in *Three Treatises*, trans. A. T. W. Steinhauser, rev. Frederick C. Ahrens and Abdel Ross Wentz (Philadelphia: Fortress Press, 1970 [1520]), 210.
39. For a discussion of this "cycle theory of violence," see Lenore Walker, *The Battered Woman* (New York: Harper & Row, 1979), 55–70.
40. Luther, *Genesis*, 68–69. Luther's construction of female nature as "weaker" continues the reasoning of the two Dominican priests who wrote the *Malleus Maleficarum*, first published in 1486; by 1520 there were fourteen known editions. The 1486 edition reads: "Since they [women] are feebler both in mind and body, it is not surprising that they should come more under the spell of witchcraft." Heinrich Kramer and James Sprenger, *Malleus Maleficarum*, trans. Montague Summers (New York: Benjamin Blom, 1970), 44. Being inferior in her ability to image God, woman was more susceptible to imaging the devil.
41. Luther, *Genesis*, 151. For an alternative interpretation of Genesis 3:1, see Phyllis Trible, *God and the Rhetoric of Sexuality* (Philadelphia: Fortress Press, 1978), 105–15.
42. Gerda Lerner notes that this argument has been "frequently subverted by feminist re-interpreters who reasoned that Eve could not help her inborn weakness and that therefore her sin was less than Adam's." Lerner, *The Creation of Feminist Consciousness: From the Middle Ages to 1870* (New York: Oxford University Press, 1993), 142. This construction of woman's nature as "weaker" caused women to suffer at the hands of legal authorities: "A woman is also to be tortured before a man whenever both sexes are put to the question, because 'she has a weak and unstable constitution,' . . . and will confess the sooner." Ian MacClean, *The Renaissance Notion of Woman: A Study in the Fortunes of Scholasticism and Medical Science in European Intellectual Life* (Cambridge: Cambridge University Press, 1980), 78.
43. Luther, *Genesis*, 199.
44. Martin Luther, *The Order of Marriage for Common Pastors*,

in *Luther's Works*, vol. 53, ed. and rev. Ulrich S. Leupold, trans. Paul Zeller Strodach (Philadelphia: Fortress Press, 1965 [1529]), 114.

45. Luther, *Genesis*, 202–3.

46. However, Kristen E. Kvam argues that Luther interprets the rule of husbands over wives and men over women as the male's punishment for sin, not God's original intent. See "The Sweat of the Brow Is of Many Kinds: Luther on the Duties of Adam and His Sons," *Currents in Theology and Mission* 24 (1997): 44–49.

47. Martin Luther, *Notes on Ecclesiastes*, in *Luther's Works*, vol. 15, ed. and trans. Jaroslav Pelikan (St. Louis, Mo.: Concordia, 1972 [1532]), 130.

48. Ibid., 131.

49. Ibid., 132.

50. Martin Luther, *Table Talk*, in *Luther's Works*, vol. 54, ed. and trans. Theodore G. Tappert (Philadelphia: Fortress Press, 1967 [1566]), 174. Luther was not the only reformer to denigrate women's ability to rule. Another obvious example is John Knox, who published "First Blast of the Trumpet against the Monstrous Regiment of Women" in 1558. Although the targets of this pamphlet were the three anti-Protestant women on the thrones of England, France, and Scotland, the pamphlet's publication coincided with the accession in England of a Protestant, Elizabeth I. Queen Elizabeth responded to Knox by "indignantly and permanently debar[ring] the rash author from her realm." *The New Encyclopaedia Britannica*, 15th ed., s.v. "John Knox." One may be assured that neither Luther nor Knox would have been amused by the current slogan "A woman's place is in the house and the senate."

51. Martin Luther, quoted in *What Luther Says: An Anthology*, vol. 3, ed. and trans. Ewald M. Plass (St. Louis, Mo.: Concordia, 1959), 1458.

52. Luther, *Table Talk*, 8. Elisabeth Schüssler Fiorenza names the "cultural and religious construction of docile feminine bodies and subservient feminine selves" as a form of "systemic" violence against women. For her analysis, see intro-

duction to *Violence against Women*, ed. Elizabeth Schüssler Fiorenza and M. Shawn Copeland, *Concilium*, no. 1 (1994): x–xiii.

53. Luther, *Genesis*, 134.

54. Eileen Power, *Medieval Women*, ed. M. M. Postan (Cambridge: Cambridge University Press, 1975), 42.

55. Hildegard's political influence can be seen in her correspondence with many of the secular and ecclesiastical leaders of her time, including Emperor Frederick Barbarossa, Queen Eleanor of Aquitaine, King Henry II, Pope Eugenius III, Pope Alexander III, and Bernard of Clairvaux. See *The Personal Correspondence of Hildegard of Bingen*, trans. Joseph L. Baird (New York: Oxford University Press, 2006). For a more extensive collection, see *The Letters of Hildegard of Bingen*, vol. 1, trans. Joseph L. Baird and Radd K. Ehrman (Los Angeles: Getty, 1998); *The Letters of Hildegard of Bingen*, vol. 2, trans. Joseph L. Baird and Radd K. Ehrman (Oxford: Oxford University Press, 1998); and *The Letters of Hildegard of Bingen*, vol. 3, trans. Joseph L. Baird and Radd K. Ehrman (New York: Oxford University Press, 2004). See also Barbara Newman, ed., *Voice of the Living Light: Hildegard of Bingen and Her World* (Berkeley: University of California Press, 1998).

56. Lyndal Roper, *The Holy Household: Women and Morals in Reformation Augsburg* (Oxford: Clarendon, 1989), 221. For a discussion of the systematic attempt to close the eight convents in Augsburg after 1537, see Roper, 206–44. Her discussion illuminates the issues of gender, class, authority, and economics involved as the city council sought to gain control of these properties.

57. Power, *Medieval Women*, 53. For further description of the activities of working women, see Power, 53–75. For a discussion of the size and importance of this sector of medieval economy, see Rodney H. Hilton, "Women Traders in Medieval England," *Women's Studies: An Interdisciplinary Journal* 11 (1984): 139–55.

58. Quoted in Julia O'Faolain and Lauro Martines, eds., *Not in God's Image* (New York: Harper & Row, 1973), 159–60.

59. Roland H. Bainton, *Here I Stand: A Life of Martin Luther* (New York: Abingdon-Cokesbury, 1950), 292.

60. The laws that forbid married clergy in the Roman Catholic Church were not established until 1139 and 1563. After 1139, priests were forbidden to marry, and after the Council of Trent (1545–1563), married men were barred from the priesthood. Uta Ranke-Heinemann, *Eunuchs for the Kingdom of Heaven: Women, Sexuality, and the Catholic Church*, trans. Peter Heinegg (New York: Penguin Books, 1990), 100. For a discussion of the violence against wives of clergy sanctioned by church officials, see Ranke-Heinemann, 109–12 and 115–16.

61. G. G. Coulton, *Medieval Panorama: The English Scene from Conquest to Reformation* (Cambridge: University Press, 1938), 615. Rosemary Radford Ruether suggests a connection between the "contempt of celibate legislators for married women" and "the fact that there crept into church law justification of the right of husbands to beat their wives." She also notes that in this same period, rabbinic law permitted a woman to request a divorce if beaten by her husband. Ruether, "The Western Religious Tradition and Violence against Women in the Home," in *Christianity, Patriarchy, and Abuse: A Feminist Critique*, ed. Joanne Carlson Brown and Carole R. Bohn (Cleveland: Pilgrim, 1989), 34. For a discussion of cases in which the Jewish court would "compel" a husband to divorce his wife because he had physically abused her, see Rachel Biale, *Women and Jewish Law: An Exploration of Women's Issues in Halakhic Sources* (New York: Schocken Books), 92–96. I am indebted to Jennifer Gubkin for bringing Biale's book to my attention.

62. Lawrence Stone, *The Family, Sex and Marriage in England, 1500–1800* (New York: Harper & Row, 1977), 326. The enduring nature of this practice is evidenced by an English cartoon published in 1782. "Judge Thumb," a large figure wearing a judicial wig and robe, carries bundles of sticks and is selling them as "a cure for a nasty wife." In the background, a wife cries, "Murder," and flees her husband, who justifies the stick he has raised over her head by saying, "It's

no bigger than my thumb." Stone, plate 19. However, due to the developing notion of the "companionate marriage" in the late eighteenth century, Stone notes there was a "great outcry" against a judge who "tried to revive" this rule in 1782. Stone, 326.

63. Coulton, *Medieval Panorama*, x, 616.

64. Quoted in ibid., 617.

65. For additional examples of the social sanction of wife abuse, see O'Faolain and Martines, *Not in God's Image*, 175–78.

66. Quoted in Stone, *Family, Sex and Marriage*, 197.

67. Martin Luther, *Sermons on the First Epistle of St. Peter*, in *Luther's Works*, vol. 30, ed. Jaroslav Pelikan, trans. Martin H. Bertram (St. Louis, Mo.: Concordia, 1967 [1523]), 88.

68. Ibid.

69. Martin Luther, quoted in *What Luther Says: An Anthology*, vol. 2, ed. and trans. Ewald M. Plass (Saint Louis, Mo.: Concordia 1959), 903.

70. Public ridicule of husbands who "indulged" their wives is illustrated in a German woodcut, c. 1533. Entitled "A Husband Who Does Not Rule," the woodcut shows the husband on his hands and knees harnessed to a cart loaded with a large wooden tub. As he pulls the cart, his wife stands over him with a whip in one hand and his sword, pants, and purse in her other hand. Steven Ozment, *When Fathers Ruled: Family Life in Reformation Europe* (Cambridge: Harvard University Press, 1983), x, 52. The wife is anything but "weak" as she holds the symbols of her husband's masculinity and authority.

On the other hand, the appeal to woman's "weaker nature" as an argument against wife beating received wide attention in England. This appeal was included in the "Homily on Marriage" that by order of the Crown (Elizabeth I) all parsons read in church every Sunday from 1562 onward. Stone, *Family, Sex and Marriage*, 198. Stone interprets the "greatest impact" of the weekly reading as reinforcing "the inferior status, rights, and character of a wife" (198). However, I suggest that perhaps Queen Elizabeth was attempting to reduce the amount of violence against wives. It would be interesting to know if Queen Elizabeth sponsored any legislation to reverse the legal sanction of abusive husbands.

71. Martin Luther, *Commentary on 1 Corinthians 7*, in *Luther's Works*, vol. 28, ed. Hilton C. Oswald, trans. Edward Sittler (St. Louis, Mo.: Concordia, 1973 [1523]), 51.

72. Luther, quoted in Plass, *What Luther Says*, vol. 2, 906.

73. Luther, *First Epistle of St. Peter*, 92.

74. Martin Luther, *The Bondage of the Will*, trans. Henry Cole (Grand Rapids: Baker, 1976 [1525]), 335.

75. Luther, quoted in Plass, *What Luther Says*, vol. 2, 903.

76. Martin Luther, quoted in Preserved Smith, *The Life and Letters of Martin Luther* (Boston: Houghton Mifflin, 1911), 180.

77. Luther, *Table Talk*, 34.

78. Luther, *Freedom of a Christian*, 290–92.

79. Martin Luther, *Against the Spiritual Estate of the Pope and Bishops, Falsely So Called*, in *Luther's Works*, vol. 39, ed. Eric W. Gritsch, trans. Eric W. and Ruth C. Gritsch (Philadelphia: Fortress Press, 1970 [1523]), 279.

80. Augustine, *Genesis*, 182–85.

81. Luther, *1 Corinthians 7*, 45.

82. The relationship between the Reformation and the reinforcement of the patriarchal family has been made by a number of scholars. See, for example, Stone, *Family, Sex and Marriage*, 151–218; and Bonnie S. Anderson and Judith P. Zinsser, *A History of Their Own: Women in Europe from Prehistory to the Present*, vol. 1 (New York: Harper & Row, 1988), 256–63. For a discussion of how the Reformation ideal of marriage supported the guilds in particular, see Roper, *Holy Household*, 7–55.

83. Anderson and Zinsser, *History of Their Own*, 256.

84. Luther's support of the traditional hierarchical structures of society is also evident in his condemnation of the German peasant revolt in 1525. See *Against the Robbing and Murdering Hordes of Peasants*, in *Luther's Works*, vol. 46, ed. Robert C. Schultz, trans. Frederick C. Ahrens (Philadelphia: Fortress Press, 1967 [1525]). I am indebted to Marit Trelstad for reminding me of this connection.

85. See *The Standard Edition of the Complete Psychological Works of Sigmund Freud*, vol. 21, ed. and trans. James Strachey (London: Hogarth, 1961), 5–56. I am grateful to Kathleen J. Greider and Helene T. Russell for critique and discussion of my analysis of Freud's work.

86. Following the English translation of James Strachey in *The Standard Edition of the Complete Psychological Works of Sigmund Freud*, I am using the word "mind." However, Bruno Bettelheim argues that Freud intended to be describing the processes of the soul, and Freud's work has been seriously distorted by the elimination of Freud's references to the soul, *die Seele*, in the English translations. Bettelheim explains: "The word that the translators substitute for 'of the soul'—'mental'—has an exact German equivalent; namely, *geistig*, which means 'of the mind,' or 'of the intellect.' If Freud had meant *geistig*, he would have written *geistig*." Bettelheim, *Freud and Man's Soul* (New York: Vintage Books, 1982), 70–71.

87. Sigmund Freud, "The Ego and the Id," in Strachey, *Complete Psychological Works*, 19:34, 54.

88. Ibid., 57. Freud also postulates a "castration complex" in women. However, in women this complex is marked by feelings of being "wronged" and "envious" rather than "fear." Freud, "Femininity," in *New Introductory Lectures on Psychoanalysis*, lecture 33, ed. and trans. James Strachey (New York: W. W. Norton, 1965 [1933]), 110–11.

89. Sigmund Freud, "Dissection of the Personality," in Strachey, *New Introductory Lectures*, lecture 31, 65.

90. Sigmund Freud, "The Question of Lay Analysis," in Strachey, *Complete Psychological Works*, 20:212.

91. Sigmund Freud, "Three Essays on Sexuality," in *The Standard Edition of the Complete Psychological Works of Sigmund Freud*, vol. 7, ed. and trans. James Strachey (London: Hogarth, 1953 [1905]), 151.

92. Sigmund Freud, "Femininity," 100.

93. Ibid., 119.

94. Susan Griffin, *Pornography and Silence: Culture's Revenge against Nature* (New York: Harper & Row, 1981), 148. For

a twentieth-century interpretation of nineteenth-century female vampires, see *Bram Stoker's Dracula*, DVD, directed by Francis Ford Coppola (1992; Sony Pictures, 1997). Based on Stoker's novel first published in 1897, the film portrays a group of men, including a doctor who works in an insane asylum, attempting to "cure" two women who have been bitten by the vampire Count Dracula. In her analysis of the novel, Elaine Showalter suggests that the treatment the two women receive from the men is representative of the attempt by late Victorian men to control the "New Woman" of the period who was perceived by the men to be sexually daring and intellectually ambitious. Elaine Showalter, *Sexual Anarchy: Gender and Culture at the Fin de Siecle* (New York: Viking, 1990), 180.

95. Freud, "Dissection," 66.

96. Freud, "Femininity," 114.

97. Augustine, *The City of God*, trans. Gerald G. Walsh, Demetrius B. Zema, Grace Monahan, and Daniel J. Honan (New York: Doubleday, 1958), 308.

98. Sigmund Freud, *Totem and Taboo: Some Points of Agreement between the Mental Lives of Savages and Neurotics*, ed. and trans. James Strachey (New York: W. W. Norton, 1950 [1912–13]), 156, 176, 178–79.

99. For an alternative analysis of the relationship between sexual desire and sin in Freud's theory, see Sharon MacIssac: "Concupiscence is no longer viewed as frustrating and disheartening evidence of the fall from Adam. It emerges for what before all else it is: a natural quality of man." MacIssac, *Freud and Original Sin* (New York: Paulist, 1974), 113.

100. Freud, *Totem and Taboo*, 190–91.

101. Freud, "Ego and Id," 38.

102. Sigmund Freud, *Moses and Monotheism*, trans. Katherine Jones (New York: Vintage Books, 1939), 104.

103. Sigmund Freud, "Some Psychical Consequences of the Anatomical Distinction between the Sexes," in Strachey, *Complete Psychological Works*, 19:252.

104. Freud, "Dissection," 58.

105. Freud, "Femininity," 112.

106. Jane Flax, *Thinking Fragments: Psychoanalysis, Feminism, and Postmodernism in the Contemporary West* (Berkeley: University of California Press, 1990), 84. Judith Van Herik explores how Freud's "theory of asymmetrical genders inform[s] his psychoanalytic criticism of . . . mental relationships to God." Van Herik, *Freud on Femininity and Faith* (Berkeley: University of California Press, 1982), 2.

107. Freud, "Some Psychical Consequences," 252.

108. Ibid.

109. Freud, "Femininity," 102.

110. Sigmund Freud, "'A Child Is Being Beaten': A Contribution to the Study of the Origin of Sexual Perversions," in Strachey, *Complete Psychological Works,* 17:189.

111. Freud, "Three Essays," 158.

112. Rosemary Radford Ruether, *New Woman, New Earth: Sexist Ideologies and Human Liberation* (New York: Seabury, 1975).

113. Other issues that women in the nineteenth century were pursuing included improved working conditions for women, the abolition of legalized prostitution, and alternatives to marriage. See Eleanor S. Riemer and John C. Fout, eds., *European Women: A Documentary History, 1789–1945* (New York: Schocken Books, 1980), 91–93, 222, and 228–30.

114. Dobash and Dobash, *Violence against Wives,* 74. Previously in 1878, Frances Power Cobbe had asserted that the cause of wife beating was the legal and social construction of the wife as property of the husband. Cobbe, "Wife Torture in England," *Contemporary Review* 32 (April–July 1878): 62, quoted in Dobash and Dobash, 73. Following the publication of Cobbe's document, the Matrimonial Causes Act Amendment Bill was passed in the same year (1878). This bill allowed for separation, but not divorce, on the grounds of cruelty; the wife was also allowed "to gain custody of the children and receive support." Yet some officials were reluctant to enforce this legislation because they thought it "might be detrimental to the husband or to the sanctity of marriage." This early legislation proved to be so ineffective that the issue of wife beating was taken up again by British

(and American) women working for the vote in the early twentieth century. Dobash and Dobash, 73–74.

In addition to questioning the law, Cobbe also challenged the use of Scripture to justify the subordination of wives to husbands. She declared that just as slavery had been denounced, so should the admonition of the husband's rule as set forth in passages such as Ephesians 5 and Colossians 3. In 1881 she wrote, "In our day, men habitually set aside this apostolic teaching, so far as it concerns masters and slaves, despots and subjects, as adapted only to a past epoch. I am at a loss to see by what right, having done so, they can claim for it authority, when it happens to refer to husbands and wives." Quoted in Donna A. Behnke, *Religious Issues in Nineteenth-Century Feminism* (Troy, N.Y.: Whitston, 1982), 130–31. In the United States, feminists who argued this position that some Scripture was not applicable to the present day included Lucretia Mott, Rev. Antoinette Brown Blackwell, and Abby Morton Diaz. Behnke, 129–30.

115. For a discussion of nineteenth-century German women moving into the public sphere and the role of religion in this movement, see Catherine M. Prelinger, *Charity, Challenge, and Change* (New York: Greenwood, 1987).

116. Juliet Mitchell, *Psychoanalysis and Feminism: Freud, Reich, Laing and Women* (New York: Vintage Books, 1974), 432.

117. Lucy Freeman and Herbert S. Stream, *Freud and Women* (New York: Continuum, 1987), 136, 201.

118. Freud, "Femininity," 114.

119. Ibid., 119.

120. Dobash and Dobash, *Violence against Wives*, 75–76.

121. I am indebted to a conversation with Linda A. Nease Sullender for this analysis of the "truth" of Freud's theory of arrested moral development in females.

122. This association of women with young children is illustrated in a poster entitled "The Vote," created by British suffrage workers c. 1911–1912. See the description of this poster in ch. 2, note 74.

123. Barbara Corrado Pope, "Angels in the Devil's Workshop: Leisured and Charitable Women in Nineteenth-Century Eng-

land and France," in *Becoming Visible: Women in European History*, ed. Renate Bridenthal and Claudia Koonz (Boston: Houghton Mifflin, 1977), 309.

124. Quoted in Freeman and Stream, *Freud and Women*, 137.

125. For example, in her article "Equal Justice for Some," Gloria Killian notes that such evidence has been admissible in the state of California only since January 1, 1992. Killian, "Equal Justice for Some," *Southern California Review of Law and Women's Studies* 2 (fall 1992): 1–5. For another contemporary discussion of the law and battered women who kill their abusers, see Gibbs, " 'Till Death Do Us Part," 38–45.

126. For example, a cartoon entitled "Overdoing It" appeared in the December 22, 1883, issue of *Punch*. Two upper-class women and a man are leaving the well-furnished home of another upper-class woman. The hostess says, "What? Going already? And in Mackintoshes? Surely you are not going to walk!" One of the women who is leaving responds, "Oh, dear no! Lord Archibald is going to take us to a dear little slum he's found out near the Minories—such a fearful place! Fourteen poor things sleeping in one bed and no window!—and the Mackintoshes are to keep out infection, you know, and hide one's diamonds, and all that!" Quoted in Pope, "Angels in the Devil's Workshop," 297.

127. For an alternative view, see Sanders Gilman, *Freud, Race, and Gender* (Princeton: Princeton University Press, 1993). Gilman argues that Freud's treatment of women was a reaction of a Jew against anti-Semitism. Gilman discusses Freud's explicit parallels between Jewishness and femaleness, and how Freud constructs the relationship between Aryans and Jews as equivalent to the relationship between men and women.

Chapter 4 Rethinking Sin

1. *Fried Green Tomatoes*, DVD, directed by Jon Avnet (1991; Universal City, Calif.: Universal Home Video, 1998).

2. I am grateful to Jack Verheyden for his review of this section at an earlier stage.

3. Friedrich Schleiermacher, *The Christian Faith*, ed. H. R. Mackintosh and J. S. Stewart, trans. D. M. Baillie et al. (Edinburgh: T. & T. Clark, 1928 [1830]), 13.
4. Ibid., 22.
5. Ibid., 17.
6. Ibid., 274.
7. Ibid., 271.
8. Ibid., 276.
9. Ibid., 307.
10. Ibid., 296.
11. Ibid.
12. Ibid., 299.
13. Ibid., 287–88.
14. Ibid., 304.
15. Ibid., 286.
16. Ibid., 307.
17. Ibid., 285.
18. Ibid., 273.
19. Ibid., 406.
20. Naming the first woman as responsible for human misery and suffering is firmly grounded in Western civilization. Paralleling the biblical story of Eve is the classical Greek tale of Pandora written by Hesiod in the sixth century B.C.E. These two stories were preceded by the Jewish story of Lilith, Adam's first wife, dating from 1000 C.E. See Aviva Cantor, "The Lilith Question," in *On Being a Jewish Feminist: A Reader*, ed. Susannah Heschel (New York: Schocken Books, 1983), 40–50.
21. Schleiermacher supported his friend Dorothea Veit when she divorced her husband after suffering his abuse. In a letter written three weeks after her divorce, Dorothea exclaimed, "Imagine how I feel—in all my life, this is the first time that I am free from the fear of having to bear an unpleasant conversation, an onerous presence, or even humiliating rudeness. . . . Schlegel, Schleiermacher, and [Henriette] Herz lent me their support." Lorely French, "Dorothea Schlegel," trans. Lorely French, in *Bitter Healing: German Women Writers from 1700–1830: An Anthology*, ed. Jeannine Blackwell

and Susanne Zantop (Lincoln: University of Nebraska Press, 1990), 340.

22. To draw upon Tillich's theological understandings of sin and sexuality as a positive resource is somewhat problematic, given Hannah Tillich's account of her husband's sexual behavior. See Hannah Tillich, *From Time to Time* (New York: Stein and Day, 1973). One can only lament the gap between Tillich's conception of sexuality as a medium of divine revelation and the abuse reported by Hannah Tillich. For a compelling analysis of this gap, see Alexander C. Irwin, *Eros toward the World: Paul Tillich and the Theology of the Erotic* (Minneapolis: Fortress Press, 1991), 99–120.

23. I am grateful to Daniel J. Peterson for his comments on this section that encouraged me to further develop my analysis of Tillich's theology.

24. Paul Tillich, *Systematic Theology*, vol. 2 (Chicago: University of Chicago Press, 1957), 35.

25. Ibid., 32.

26. Ibid., 33–34.

27. Ibid., 35–36.

28. Ibid., 44, 46.

29. For an extended critique of Tillich's theology as not recognizing both human and divine existence as relational, see Carter Heyward, *Touching Our Strength: The Erotic as Power and the Love of God* (San Francisco: Harper & Row, 1989), 63–67.

30. However, Tillich's understanding of Providence as "a creative and saving possibility implied in every situation" is similar to the relational worldview of God as process. See Paul Tillich, "The Meaning of Providence," in *The Shaking of the Foundations* (New York: Charles Scribner's Sons, 1948), 106. For a critique of Tillich's understanding of God from a process-relational worldview, see Charles Hartshorne, "Tillich's Doctrine of God," in *The Theology of Paul Tillich*, ed. Charles W. Kegley and Robert W. Bretall (New York: Macmillan, 1952), 164–95. For Tillich's reply, see pp. 334–35 and 339–40 in the same volume.

31. Judith Plaskow, *Sex, Sin and Grace: Women's Experience and the Theologies of Reinhold Niebuhr and Paul Tillich* (Lanham,

Md.: University Press of America, 1980); Valerie Saiving Goldstein, "The Human Situation: A Feminine View," *Journal of Religion* 40 (April 1960): 100–112. Susan Nelson has developed the notion that self-denial or "hiding" is the primary sin of women in *Beyond Servanthood: Christianity and the Liberation of Women* (Lanham, Md.: University Press of America, 1989).

32. Plaskow, *Sex, Sin and Grace*, 146. For Plaskow's discussion of ambiguity in Tillich's doctrine of sin regarding its relevance to women's experiences, see pp. 109–20.

33. Mary Daly and Jane Caputi, *Websters' First New Intergalactic Wickedary of the English Language* (Boston: Beacon, 1987), 87.

34. As discussed in chapter 3, Karen Jo Torjesen analyzes how women gained honor through self-denial in Greco-Roman and early Christian communities because "a woman's honor is her shame." See *When Women Were Priests: Women's Leadership in the Early Church and the Scandal of Their Subordination in the Rise of Christianity* (New York: HarperSanFrancisco, 1993), 135–52. Plaskow associates women's passivity with virtue (*Sex, Sin and Grace*, 120).

35. Tillich, *Systematic Theology*, vol. 2, 35.

36. Paul Tillich, *The Courage to Be* (New Haven, Conn.: Yale University Press, 1952), 3. For Christians, this courage is supported by participating in the "New Being" in Jesus Christ, which is the power that "has conquered existential estrangement in himself and in everyone who participates in him." Tillich, *Systematic Theology*, vol. 2, 125.

37. Daly and Caputi, *Wickedary*, 70.

38. Elizabeth A. Stanko, *Intimate Intrusions: Women's Experience of Male Violence* (London: Unwin Hyman, 1985), 56.

39. For another positive analysis of the possibilities of Tillich's understanding of *eros* for feminist and womanist theologies, see Irwin, *Eros toward the World*, 153–96.

40. Paul Tillich, *Systematic Theology*, vol. 1 (Chicago: University of Chicago Press, 1951), 119n.

41. See, for example, James B. Nelson, *Embodiment: An Approach to Sexuality and Christian Theology* (Minneapo-

lis: Augsburg Publishing House, 1978); James B. Nelson, *Between Two Gardens: Reflections on Sexuality and Religious Experience* (New York: Pilgrim, 1983); and Carter Heyward, *Touching Our Strength: The Erotic as Power and the Love of God* (San Francisco: Harper & Row, 1989). More recently, see Kelly Brown Douglas, *Sexuality and the Black Church: A Womanist Perspective* (Maryknoll, N.Y.: Orbis, 1999); Melanie A. May, *A Body Knows: A Theopoetics of Death and Resurrection* (New York: Continuum, 1995); and biblical scholar David M. Carr, *The Erotic Word: Sexuality, Spirituality, and the Bible* (Oxford: Oxford University Press, 2003).

42. Tillich, *Systematic Theology*, vol. 2, 52–54.

43. Ibid., 47.

44. Marjorie Hewitt Suchocki, *The Fall to Violence: Original Sin in Relational Theology* (New York: Crossroad, 1994), 22–23.

45. I am indebted to Patricia O'Connell Killen and Marit A. Trelstad for their responses to an earlier draft of this section that helped me clarify my ideas.

46. Suchocki, *Fall to Violence*, 12, 13, 16.

47. Ibid., 95–97.

48. Ibid., 18.

49. Ibid., 17.

50. Darien B. Cooper, *You Can Be the Wife of a Happy Husband: Discovering the Key to Marital Success* (Colorado Springs: Chariot Victor, 1974), 63. The popularity of this book is indicated by the publication of a revised and updated edition in 2005. I am indebted to Julie Neufer for locating the source of the "divine order" image.

51. Suchocki, *Fall to Violence*, 18.

52. Del Martin, *Battered Wives* (San Francisco: Glide, 1976), 3.

53. Ibid., 2.

54. Stanko, *Intimate Intrusions*, 56.

55. Suchocki, *Fall to Violence*, 84–85.

56. Ibid., 85.

57. Ibid., 90.

58. Ibid., 94–95.

59. Ibid., 92n5.

60. Ibid.
61. Ibid., 109.
62. Ibid., 99.
63. Ibid., 83.
64. Jeanne James, "The First Wednesday in June," photocopy to author, 1995.
65. Suchocki, *Fall to Violence*, 98.
66. Stanko, *Intimate Intrusions*, 54.
67. Suchocki, *Fall to Violence*, 113.
68. Ibid., 123–24.
69. Ibid., 113.
70. R. Emerson Dobash and Russell Dobash, *Violence against Wives: A Case against Patriarchy* (New York: Free Press, 1979), 33–34.
71. Martin, *Battered Wives*, 3.
72. Suchocki, *Fall to Violence*, 118.
73. Statistic from House of Ruth, Inc., P.O. Box 457, Claremont, CA 91711. March of Dimes, 1992, cited in "Domestic Violence Fact Sheet," 2008, http://www.athealth.com/Consumer/Disorders/DomViolFacts.html (August 4, 2008).
74. This view of inherited sin is shared by many liberation theologians. See, for example, Emilie Townes, ed., *A Troubling in My Soul: Womanist Perspectives on Evil and Suffering* (Maryknoll, N.Y.: Orbis Books, 1993); and Gustavo Gutiérrez, *Essential Writings*, ed. James B. Nickoloff (Maryknoll, N.Y.: Orbis Books, 1996).
75. For discussions of this view of God's power, evil, and sin, see David Ray Griffin, *God, Power, and Evil: A Process Theodicy* (Philadelphia: Westminster, 1976); and Wendy Farley, *Tragic Vision and Divine Compassion: A Contemporary Theodicy* (Louisville, Ky.: Westminster John Knox, 1990).
76. Rita Nakashima Brock has developed the concept of sin as damage to the self. See especially pp. 7–9 in *Journeys by Heart: A Christology of Erotic Power* (New York: Crossroad, 1991).

Chapter 5 Body, Sex, and Soul

1. *Like Water for Chocolate*, DVD, directed by Alfonso Arau (1993; Burbank, Calif.: Touchstone Home Entertainment, 2000). See also Laura Esquivel, *Like Water for Chocolate: A Novel in Monthly Installments with Recipes, Romances, and Home Remedies*, trans. Carol and Thomas Christensen (New York: Doubleday, 1992), 32, 40, 57.

2. For an extended discussion of this devaluation of women, the body, and sexuality, see Rosemary Radford Ruether, "Misogynism and Virginal Feminism in the Fathers of the Church," in *Religion and Sexism: Images of Woman in the Jewish and Christian Traditions*, ed. Rosemary Radford Ruether (New York: Simon & Schuster, 1974), 150–83.

3. My definition of "soul" follows Alfred North Whitehead's understanding. The soul represents the integration of the human being's experiences in this life. This understanding of soul does not address the question of immortality. I use "soul" in the position developed in this chapter for two reasons. First, I want to retain the classical understanding of the soul as including passion because I associate passion with energy; as discussed in this chapter, both body and soul are composed of energy. Second, I prefer "soul" to "mind" because of the close association of "mind" with rationality in modern Western philosophy. I am indebted to John Petersen for stimulating conversation about my use of "soul."

4. See, for example, Penelope Washbourn, "Religion and Sexuality in Contemporary Perspective, or Listening between the Bedposts," *Iliff Review* 35 (1978): 65–76; Virginia Ramey Mollenkott, *Sensuous Spirituality: Out from Fundamentalism* (New York: Crossroad, 1992); Joan H. Timmerman, *Sexuality and Spiritual Growth* (New York: Crossroad, 1992); James B. Nelson and Sandra P. Longfellow, eds., *Sexuality and the Sacred: Sources for Theological Reflection* (Louisville, Ky.: Westminster John Knox, 1994); Evelyn Eaton Whitehead and James D. Whitehead, *The Wisdom of the Body: Making Sense of Our Sexuality* (New York: Crossroad, 2001); and

David M. Carr, *The Erotic Word: Sexuality, Spirituality, and the Bible* (Oxford: Oxford University Press, 2003); Anthony B. Pinn and Dwight N. Hopkins, eds. *Loving the Body: Black Religious Studies and the Erotic* (New York: Palgrave Mac-Millan, 2004); and Miguel A. De La Torre, *A Lily Among the Thorns: Imagining a New Christian Sexuality* (San Francisco: Jossey-Bass, 2007).

5. For further discussion of how the doctrine of the incarnation influenced the development of Christian ideas about the body, see Paula M. Cooey, "The Redemption of the Body: Post-Patriarchal Reconstruction of Inherited Christian Doctrine," in *After Patriarchy: Feminist Transformations of the World Religions*, ed. Paula M. Cooey, William R. Eakin, and Jay B. McDaniel (Maryknoll, N.Y.: Orbis Books, 1991), 106–30.

6. C. Hugh Hildesley, *Journeying with Juian* (Harrisburg, Pa.: Morehouse, 1993), 17.

7. "This [being dead to the world] was emphasized by the celebration of a requiem mass for the anchorite, by the burial of the anchorite into his or her anchorhold with the sprinkling of earth, and by the bolting of the entrance to the cell, whose prison like qualities included its size, approximately twelve feet square, and the sparseness of the prescribed furnishings." See Hildesley, *Journeying*, 62.

8. Julian of Norwich, *Julian of Norwich: Showings*, trans. Edmund Colledge and James Walsh (New York: Paulist, 1978), 134.

9. Ibid., 186.

10. Ibid., 312.

11. Ibid., 186.

12. Ibid.

13. Ibid., 291.

14. Ibid., 282.

15. Ibid., 286–87.

16. Ibid., 312–13.

17. Ibid., 287.

18. Ibid., 287–88.

19. Eleanor McLaughlin, "The Christian Past: Does It Hold a Future for Women?" in *Womanspirit Rising: A Feminist*

Reader in Religion, ed. Carol P. Christ and Judith Plaskow (San Francisco: Harper & Row, 1979), 105.

20. Julian, *Showings*, 279.

21. Ibid., 293.

22. Ibid., 184, 186.

23. Friedrich Schleiermacher, *The Christian Faith*, ed. H. R. Mackintosh and J. S. Stewart, trans. D. M. Baillie et al. (Edinburgh: T. & T. Clark, 1928 [1830]), 21.

24. Ibid., 233–34.

25. Ibid., 240.

26. Ibid., 238–39.

27. Paul Tillich, *Systematic Theology*, vol. 2 (Chicago: University of Chicago Press, 1957), 36.

28. Paul Tillich, *Systematic Theology*, vol. 1 (Chicago: University of Chicago Press, 1951), 250.

29. Ibid., 235.

30. Ibid., 118.

31. Ibid.

32. Ibid., 119n. For a discussion of these symbols as related to women, see Margaret R. Miles, *Carnal Knowing: Female Nakedness and Religious Meaning in the Christian West* (Boston: Beacon, 1989).

33. Ibid. Current Protestant thinkers have responded to Tillich's concern, daring to write theology from sexual experience. Two well-known examples include Carter Heyward, *Touching Our Strength: The Erotic as Power and the Love of God* (San Francisco: Harper & Row, 1989); and James B. Nelson, *Embodiment: An Approach to Sexuality and Christian Theology* (Minneapolis: Augsburg Publishing House, 1978). More recent publications include Marcella Althaus-Reid, ed., *Liberation Theology and Sexuality* (Burlington, Vt.: Ashgate, 2006); Elizabeth Stuart, *Gay and Lesbian Theologies: Repetitions with Critical Difference* (Burlington, Vt.: Ashgate, 2003); and Lisa Isherwood, ed., *The Good News of the Body: Sexual Theology and Feminism* (Sheffield, UK: Sheffield Academic, 2001).

34. A similar argument is made by German Martinez and Lyn Burr Brignoli when they write, "In marriage, the sexual act for people of faith becomes a way to know God, not

through 'ideas,' but through experience; we meet the body of God with our bodies." See "Models of Marriage: A New Theological Interpretation," in *Perspectives on Marriage: A Reader*, 2nd ed., ed. Kieran Scott and Michael Warren (New York: Oxford University Press, 2001), 76.

35. Rebecca Parker, "Making Love as a Means of Grace," *World: The Journal of the Unitarian Universalist Association* 8 (July–August 1994): 23.

36. Ibid., 24.

37. Ibid.

38. Ibid.

39. Ibid.

40. Ibid., 23.

41. Alfred North Whitehead, *Process and Reality, Corrected Edition*, ed. David Ray Griffin and Donald W. Sherburne (New York: Free Press, 1978 [1929]), 18.

42. Most experiences are subconscious because Whitehead believes that experience precedes consciousness in the development of being. For example, a rock has experiences because it exists, but not consciousness.

43. For further discussion of Whitehead's philosophy of the relationship between body and soul, see John B. Cobb Jr., *Postmodernism and Public Policy: Reframing Religion, Culture, Education, Sexuality, Class, Race, Politics, and the Economy* (Albany: State University of New York Press, 2002), 86–89.

44. David Ray Griffin, "The Importance of Being Human: A Postmodern Vision," in *God and Religion in the Postmodern World: Essays in Postmodern Theology*, ed. David Ray Griffin (Albany: State University of New York Press, 1989), 23.

45. Ibid., 23–24.

46. For a discussion of the social construction of the body in Western history, see Anthony Synnott, "Tomb, Temple, Machine and Self: The Social Construction of the Body," *British Journal of Sociology* 43, no. 1 (1992): 79–110.

47. The notion of the body as the receptacle for a fully developed soul has political implications. For example, to promote their cause, antiabortion activists have used the belief that the

fetus has a soul from the moment of conception. For example, see Uta Ranke-Heinemann, *Eunuchs for the Kingdom of Heaven* (New York: Penguin, 1991), 304–6. The position I am developing opposes this cause.

48. Alfred North Whitehead, *Adventures of Ideas* (New York: Free Press, 1961 [1933]), 275.

49. Alfred North Whitehead, *Modes of Thought* (New York: Free Press, 1968 [1938]), 211.

50. Whitehead, *Process and Reality*, 311–12.

51. Whitehead, *Modes of Thought*, 162.

52. Ibid., 163.

53. Washbourn, "Religion and Sexuality," 66–67.

54. Joe Holland, "A Postmodern Vision of Spirituality and Society," in *Spirituality and Society: Postmodern Visions*, ed. David Ray Griffin (Albany: State University of New York Press, 1988), 51.

55. Susan Griffin, *Pornography and Silence: Culture's Revenge against Nature* (New York: Harper & Row, 1981), 3.

56. Pamela Cooper-White, *The Cry of Tamar: Violence against Women and the Church's Response* (Minneapolis: Fortress Press, 1995), 19.

57. Audre Lorde, *Sister Outsider: Essays and Speeches* (Trumansburg, N.Y.: Crossing, 1984), 51. Although I am using the quotation from Lorde in my discussion of sexual energy, Lorde defines the "erotic" in a much broader sense as "an assertion of the lifeforce of women; of that creative energy empowered" (55).

Chapter 6 Marriage and Social Change

1. Antoine de Saint-Exupéry, *Wind, Sand and Stars*, trans. Lewis Galantière (New York: Harcourt Brace, 1939), quoted in *A Guide for Grown-ups: Essential Wisdom from the Collected Works of Antoine de Saint-Exupéry* (San Diego, New York, and London: Harcourt, 2002), 28.

2. Rosemary Radford Ruether, *New Woman, New Earth: Sexist Ideologies and Human Liberation* (New York: Seabury Press, 1975), 210–11.

3. See, for example, Lyndal Roper, *The Holy Household: Women and Morals in Reformation Augsburg* (Oxford: Clarendon, 1989); Steven Ozment, *When Fathers Ruled: Family Life in Reformation Europe* (Cambridge and London: Harvard University Press, 1983); and Rosemary Haughton, *The Theology of Marriage* (Hales Corners, Wis.: Clergy Book Service, 1971), 53.

4. For alternative visions of the marriage ideal, see John K. Tarwater, *Marriage as Covenant: Considering God's Design at Creation and the Contemporary Moral Consequences* (Lanham, Md.: University Press of America, 2006); John P. Bartkowski, *Remaking the Godly Marriage: Gender Negotiation in Evangelical Families* (New Brunswick, N.J.: Rutgers University Press, 2003); and David Popenoe, "Modern Marriage: Revising the Cultural Script," in Michael S. Kimmel, ed., with Amy Aronson, *The Gendered Society Reader*, 2nd ed. (New York and Oxford: Oxford University Press, 2004), 170–86.

5. Marie M. Fortune, "Someone You Know Is Suffering from the Trauma and Pain of Sexual or Domestic Violence. How Have Religious Communities Responded?" (Seattle: Center for the Prevention of Sexual and Domestic Violence, 1995).

6. Four excellent resources that address how the church should respond to violence against women are Monica A. Coleman, *The Dinah Project: A Handbook for Congregational Response to Sexual Violence* (Cleveland, Ohio: Pilgrim, 2004); Nancy Nason-Clark, *The Battered Wife: How Christians Confront Family Violence* (Louisville, Ky.: Westminster John Knox, 1997); Pamela Cooper-White, *The Cry of Tamar: Violence against Women and the Church's Response* (Minneapolis: Fortress Press, 1995); and Carol J. Adams, *Woman-Battering* (Minneapolis: Fortress Press, 1994).

7. One resource for raising awareness about domestic violence, workplace violence, and economic justice for women is the film *North Country*, DVD, directed by Niki Caro (2005; Warner Home Video, 2006). This film is based on the story of the first group of women to win a class-action lawsuit

against their employer for sexual harassment. Their case became the basis for the current laws against sexual harassment in the U.S. Due to its R rating, this film is most appropriate for college-age and other adult groups.

8. See Walter Wink's analysis of Jesus' teachings to "turn the other cheek" and "go the second mile" in *The Powers That Be: Theology for a New Millennium* (New York: Doubleday, 1998), 98–111, 206. Wink names "Jesus' Third Way" as a way of resistance that is neither violent nor passive.

9. Two examples are the Samaritan woman who is living with a man who is not her husband (John 4:7–39) and the woman caught in adultery (John 8:3–11).

10. Here I am joining with other process theologians who make this point. See John B. Cobb Jr., *Matters of Life and Death* (Louisville, Ky.: Westminster John Knox Press, 1991), 118–20; and Mary Ellen Kilsby, John B. Cobb Jr., and William A. Beardslee, "What Shall the Church Say about Homosexuality?" in *Now What's a Christian to Do?* ed. David Polk (St. Louis, Mo.: Chalice Press, 1994), 73–100.

11. Marjorie Hewitt Suchocki, *The End of Evil: Process Eschatology in Historical Context* (Albany: State University of New York Press, 1988), 75.

12. Bernard Loomer, "Two Conceptions of Power," *Process Studies* 6, no. 1 (spring 1976): 26.

ACKNOWLEDGMENTS

I am happy to acknowledge prior work in which I have developed the ideas in this book:

Portions of Chapters 1, 2, 5, and 6 originally published as "Process Perspectives on Sexuality, Love, and Marriage." In *Handbook of Process Theology*, eds. Jay McDaniel and Donna Bowman, 120–35. St. Louis, Mo.: Chalice Press, 2006.

Portions of Chapters 1, 2, 5, and 6 orginally published as "Marriage after Patriarchy?" *Creative Transformations* 8:3 (Spring 1999). 6-9, 22.

Portion of Chapter 5 originally published as "Dualism without Domination: A Reinterpretation of Dualism for Ecofeminist Theory." In *Constructing a Relational Cosmology*, ed. Paul O. Ingram, 54–68. Eugene, Ore.: Pickwick Publications, 2006.

Portions of Chapter 1 and 6 originally published as "Marriage after Patriarchy? Partner Relationships and Public Religion" in *Religion in a Pluralistic Age: Proceedings of the Third International Conference on Philosophical Theology*. Donald A. Crosby and Charley D. Hardwick, eds. Peter Lang Press, 2001. 71–81.

Portions of Chapters 4 and 5 originally published as "Don't Blame It on the Seeds: Toward a Feminist Process Understanding of Anthropology, Sin, and Sexuality," *Process Studies* 22:2 (Summer 1993). 71–83.

INDEX